May [illegible]

these pleasures [illegible]

which are a part of our traditions

the Gallic Food-lover

Jérôme

(and still incapable of cooking

though)

Claudine DULUAT - Martin CANTEGRIT

# RECIPES & WINES

## from

# BURGUNDY

Translated by Juliet Scott-Freyche

LES ÉDITIONS DU LAQUET

# Preface

Burgundy in a book. Nothing less pardoxical, since two of its most precious jewels are to be savoured : its gastronomy and its great wines, both inherited from age-old traditions.

Two arts, should I say, which are not only the expression of the exceptional personality of a land, chosen by the Gods perhaps, but also, through fame, universally accessible.

So many people all over the world now hold Burgundy in their hearts forever, and today it is an immense pleasure for me to open this book for you. Indulge yourselves !

We owe it to two great connaisseurs — Claudine Duluat, born and brought up in Burgundy, whose pen is without equal in gathering traditional Burgundy recipes and reproducing them in all their authenticity, thus helping to preserve and promote our national heritage (she is also the author of other works such as «A hundred ways with terrines») and Martin Cantegrit, self-taught expert on Burgundy wines, who has been masterminding the restaurant Le Récamier brilliantly for twenty years, where the charm of the welcome, an old-fashioned setting, and the quality of the food and wine make it one of the places where life is a pleasure. Dishes created at Le Récamier delight the palates of his Parliamentary customers (halfway between their respective Assemblies), literary figures, journalists or publishers... etc and his wine cellar honours the most demanding of them.

In «Recipes and Wines from Burgundy» Claudine Duluat and Martin Cantegrit succeed in reaching a refined and delicate balance — an alchemy of talent and work — through which the dishes add to the savour of the wines and the wine enhances the dish.

A most perfect gastronomic alliance from which, dear reader, you will take infinite pleasure.

My heart leaps at the thought of a Charolais rib of beef with morel mushrooms, married for the occasion to a Nuits-Saint-Georges 1er cru les Forêts Saint Georges 1991. How can I hold back my taste buds when faced with a Coq au vin complemented by a Clos de Vougeot 1991, faced with...

Sight for sore eyes, treat for the senses, anthology of taste, this book celebrates a certain art of living : a wine of high quality tantalizes the spirit and a dish of high quality is bliss for the stomach, thus achieving a perfect harmony between material and spiritual matters.

As the great Saint Francis of Sales said, « the body must be cared for so the soul can be happy there ».

Happy tasting !

Bernard Barbier
*Senator and Mayor of Nuits-Saint-Georges*

# Introduction

## *A subtle union of gastronomy and the land.*

If customs, language and dress change from one canton to another, Burgundy is none the less gastronomically renowned, as much for its cuisine as for its wines.

Burgundy Potée is generous, made for those with good appetites. Tradition has it that this dish should be eaten at the end of the wine harvests, when it is called " kill-dog " or " paulée " ...

However, this cuisine is also skilful, subtle and delicate. All kinds of chickens are prepared in ten exquisite ways and are universally reputed, as is the Charolais cow among beef.

Game birds and animals are still abundant in the Morvan and Bresse areas, the marshes of Doubs are rich in woodcock ; streams and rivers are always abundantly supplied with pike and trout.

Living tradition, with typically Burgundian Gougères, and Parsleyed ham which just must be served at Easter, but also gastronomy, with the famous Crayfish in Chablis or with Nantua sauce, and Dijon Pike Mousse...

Mouth-watering recipes and prestigious wines, cuisine for special days, or for every day, from Bresse to Morvan, through Guiche and Beaune, Burgundy reveals here all the secrets of an area which is inextricably linked with food and nature.

In order to make a success of Burgundy cuisine, recipes must be followed step by step, while at the same time being able to get around the difficulties in certain dishes. One of the best modern secrets is the use of a good food processor like the Magimix, which, originating from Burgundy, will soon be a part of new culinary traditions.

# Introduction

## *Wine in Burgundy*

One does not need to like wine to realise that Burgundy wines, the most surprising in France, are a work of art to be compared with the Acropolis or Chartres cathedral. Moreover, they are like a Byzantine mosaïc. There is certainly no other area in the world where farmers know their land so well ; producing great wines does not only depend on the soil, but also the slope of the land, altitude and wind. It has been discovered that all the grand crus are produced at an average altitude of 270 m on east-facing ground.

Defining climates is carried out with such great precision and has been for so long that one can imagine that Gallo-Roman wines and monks in the Middle Ages must have tasted the earth, in the same way as we now taste wine. On these fallow lands, covered with forests, without any geological knowledge or chemical analysis, they positioned their crus to a centimetre. Burgundy vineyards were built with the same infallible exactitude as cathedrals. Romanée-Conti, jewel of Burgundy red wines, is produced on 18 050 square metres (a much smaller area than the Place de la Concorde in Paris). This vineyard has not been enlarged by so much as ten centimetres since Madame de Pompadour wrangled with the Prince of Conti over it. Up to now, all scientific progress has proved incapable of modifying a single line of this magical puzzle.

Let us hope that it will remain like this for a very long time !

*For the following recipes :* ★ red wine
☆ white wine

# SOUPS

*Traditionally, a meal in Burgundy is not complete without soup...*

*Soup includes an extremely varied range of superb and rich brews : spring soup, soup with herbs, but also winter soups of which the best example is the good old cabbage soup which often made up supper alone, followed by a few local cheeses...*

*This soup is still eaten all over Burgundy.*

# POTAGE DE LA SAÔNE

## SOUP FROM THE SAÔNE

Preparation **45 min** Cooking time **3 hrs** Equipment **large saucepan**

Serves 6

1.8 kg fish (pike, carp, perch, tench and bream)
2 leeks
3 carrots
1 large onion stuck with 2 cloves
1 handful of cooking salt
50 g of butter
1 dessertspoon single cream
salt
freshly ground pepper
30 small toasted croutons

Clean the fish carefully, cut into cubes, then put into the saucepan, cover with water, add the cooking salt, bring to the boil, skim the surface several times.

Peel the vegetables, add to the fish in the saucepan and leave to simmer for 3 hours.

After 3 hours, blend to a smooth consistency with your Magimix, pour back into the saucepan, add a knob of butter and some freshly ground pepper. Warm through gently, while putting the croutons into a frying pan with the rest of the butter until they are golden brown.

Pour the cream into a soup tureen and stir in the soup gradually.

Sprinkle a few croutons on the top and serve immediately, with the rest of the croutons on the side.

# POTAGE DU MORVAN

## SOUP FROM THE MORVAN AREA

Preparation **25 min** Cooking time **40 min** Equipment **large saucepan**

SERVES 6

2 leeks
2 potatoes
2 turnips
2 carrots
1 small cabbage
300 g bacon
salt
freshly ground pepper
farmhouse bread

Peel the vegetables, dice them and place in the saucepan.

Cover with plenty of water, add salt, bring to the boil, then leave to simmer for 40 minutes.

Meanwhile, cut the bacon into small cubes and put into a small pan to cook gently.

When the bacon fat has melted, strain and add to the saucepan 15 minutes before serving.

Cut about fifteen thin slices of bread, place them in a soup tureen, pour in the soup and serve immediately.

# SOUPE AUX CHOUX

## CABBAGE SOUP

Preparation **20 min** Cooking time **2 hrs** Equipment **large saucepan**

SERVES 6

- 1 cabbage
- 350 g streaky bacon
- 1 dessertspoon of lard
- 1 large onion
- 2 l water
- 6 egg yolks
- 10 cl single cream
- grilled croutons
- salt
- freshly ground pepper

Remove the outer leaves of the cabbage and cut it up roughly. Peel the onion and cut it into quarters. Cut the bacon into cubes and cook them until sizzling in the saucepan with the lard. Next add the cabbage and the onion, and pour over the water.

Bring to the boil and leave to cook for 2 hours.

Meanwhile, grill the croutons.

Mix the cream and the egg yolks in a soup tureen, then, stirring constantly, pour in the soup gradually. Add the croutons, stir quickly and serve immediately.

# POTAGE AUX LENTILLES

## LENTIL SOUP

Preparation **25 min** Cooking time **35 min** Equipment **large saucepan, soup tureen**

Serves 6

500 g lentils (green lentils from Le Puy)
1 litre stock (preferably fatty)
1 onion
1 dessertspoon single cream
20 small croutons baked in the oven
1 bunch of chopped chervil
salt
freshly ground pepper

Rinse the lentils in cool water, cover with the stock, then cook in a pan with the onion for 35 minutes.

Next, drain the lentils (keep the stock) and blend them in a food processor, adding the stock through the funnel to thin the soup.

Pour the soup back into the pan and heat thoroughly.

Meanwhile, cut bread into small cubes for the croutons and bake until golden brown in the oven. Then, put the croutons into the soup tureen and cover with cream.

Pour in the soup, stir quickly, sprinkle with chervil and serve immediately.

# SOUPE À L'OIGNON CRÈME

## CREAM OF ONION SOUP

Preparation **20 min** Cooking time **30 min** Equipment **thick-based pan**

SERVES 6

3 carefully chosen onions
30 g butter
1 l of fatty stock (or 2 stock cubes)
150 g Gruyère cheese
2 egg yolks
12 thin slices of farmhouse bread
salt
freshly ground pepper

Grate the cheese, put to one side.

Peel and finely chop the onions, then brown in the pan with the butter.

Let them brown without burning, pour in the stock and cook over a low heat for 30 minutes, add salt and pepper.

Meanwhile, slice the bread thinly and use to line a soup tureen. Cover with grated gruyère and top with a knob of butter.

In a bowl, whisk the egg yolks, and whisking continually, mix in a little soup, then pour into the tureen and add the rest of the soup. Check the seasoning and serve immediately.

# VELOUTÉ D'ÉCREVISSES

## CRAYFISH VELOUTÉ

Preparation **25 min** Cooking time **35 min** Equipment **large saucepan**

SERVES 6

16 crayfish
2 l court-bouillon
1/2 bottle Pouilly Vinzelles wine
3 egg yolks
25 cl of single cream
salt
freshly ground pepper
15 croutons and 35 g butter

Clean the crayfish.

Pour the court-bouillon and the white wine into the saucepan, add salt and pepper, bring to the boil and leave to simmer for a few minutes. Then put the crayfish into the court-bouillon to cook for 10 to 15 minutes.

Next, take out the crayfish, (keep the court-bouillon) shell and remove the heads.

Blend the soup thoroughly with your Magimix to obtain a smooth purée, mix into it a litre of court-bouillon, stir well and put back onto the heat.

Meanwhile, whisk the egg yolks and cream together in a soup tureen, and stirring constantly, add the soup gradually. Check the seasoning (which should be quite spicy). Serve with the croutons which should have been fried in butter.

# SOUPE VIGNERONNE DE JEANNE

## AUNTIE JOAN'S VINEYARD SOUP

Preparation **25 min** Cooking time **40 min** Equipment **2 saucepans 1 large, 1 small**

SERVES 6

2 medium carrots
2 leeks
1 turnip
1 onion
25 g butter
1 l stock (beef with the fat skimmed off)
1/2 l red Mâcon wine
3 dessertspoons vermicelli
salt
freshly ground pepper

Peel all the vegetables, then cut them into thin slices or chop them.

Next, put them into the large saucepan and cook slowly with the butter over a low heat. Leave for 10 minutes, stirring regularly.

Meanwhile, pour the wine into the other pan, bring it to the boil and reduce to half, then pour it over the vegetables. Next add the hot stock, mix well, add a little salt and pepper, cover and leave to simmer for another twenty minutes.

Take off the lid and sprinkle the vermicelli over the liquid slowly, mix well, cook for 10 minutes stirring regularly, and serve immediately.

# VELOUTÉ CHAROLAIS

Preparation **10 min** Cooking time **20 min** Equipment **large saucepan**

SERVES 6

| | |
|---|---|
| 1.5 l calf's head stock | 3 egg yolks |
| 1 dl cold milk | 10 cl single cream |
| 10 cl creamed rice | salt |
| 2 dessertspoons tapioca | freshly ground pepper |

Bring the veal stock to the boil, keep it on one side.

Meanwhile, thin down the creamed rice with the cold milk, then pour into the stock, mix well and sprinkle with the tapioca slowly, while stirring constantly. Leave to simmer for 20 minutes. Whisk the egg yolks and the cream together in a soup tureen, mix well, then while stirring, add the velouté gradually. Season to taste and serve immediately.

# Starters

*Today, hors-d'oeuvres*
*and starters are grouped together*
*and are becoming more and more diversified,*
*especially in Burgundy...*

*From a simple appetizer like Gougère,*
*or the robust Matefaim, a kind of thick pancake*
*with fines herbes, to the refined and famous*
*Crayfish in Chablis, through subtle snail cassolettes*
*(snail, King of Burgundy)*
*not forgetting parsleyed ham,*
*whose preparation is truly spectacular...*

*Starters are the prelude to a good meal.*

# ÉCREVISSES AU VIN BLANC

## CRAYFISH IN WHITE WINE

Preparation **30 min** Cooking time **15 min** Equipment **large saucepan**

SERVES 6

| | |
|---|---|
| 1 kg crayfish | 20 cl single cream |
| 1 l Pouilly wine | 1 large bunch of chopped chervil |
| 1 l water | salt |
| 3 sprigs thyme | freshly ground pepper |
| 1 bay leaf | |

Pour the wine and the water into the saucepan, add the thyme and bay leaf, salt and pepper, then bring to the boil and simmer for 30 minutes.

Next, put the crayfish into this court-bouillon, and cook for 15 minutes.

Using a draining spoon, take out the crayfish and place on a large dish, keeping them hot. Reduce the court-bouillon by half, add the cream, and leave to simmer for a few minutes. Check the seasoning which should be quite spicy, and pour the sauce over the crayfish. Sprinkle with chervil and serve immediately.

☆☆ CHÂTEAU FUISSÉ 1991 - J.J. Vincent et Fils

*This delicate Pouilly Fuissé possesses a fine acidity which allows it to be served without any risks with many dishes. It suits lemony and fish dishes perfectly.*

# ŒUFS EN MEURETTE

## EGGS IN A WINE SAUCE

Preparation **1 hr 30 min** Cooking time **3 to 4 min**
Equipment **saucepans, deep frying pan, and frying pan**

SERVES 6

12 eggs
6 slices of bread
150 g of streaky bacon
250 g button mushrooms
60 g butter
60 g flour
21/4 l red wine
1/2 l veal stock
2 large veal bones
2 carrots
3 onions
1 head of garlic
table salt
cooking salt
peppercorns
ground pepper
bouquet garni (parsley, tarragon, thyme, bay leaf, stick of celery)
1 stock cube or a sachet of veal stock

Pour a half litre of water into a saucepan, add the stock cube or sachet of veal stock, bring to the boil and put aside.

Meanwhile, peel the vegetables, cut the carrots into large pieces, the onions and the head of garlic in half. Prepare the bouquet garni. Clean the mushrooms and cut them into pieces.

Cut the bacon into small cubes, then cream the butter by hand with the flour to obtain a smooth paste.

Next, put the veal bones and remaining onion onto a very hot baking tin. Cook until brown, almost black, for about 15 minutes.

While this is cooking, pour 1/4 litre of water into a saucepan and add salt, pepper, lemon juice and a knob of butter. Bring to the boil, then add the mushrooms and cook for a further 15 minutes.

Then take the veal bones and onion out of the oven, put them into a saucepan with the flavourings (carrots, onions, bouquet garni, head of garlic, cooking salt and crushed peppercorns), then add 1 1/2 litres of red wine and the veal stock and cook over a high heat.

Add 1/4 litre of mushroom juice, then leave to cook for at least an hour.

During this time, blanch and then fry the bacon with the mushrooms, a clove of garlic and a knob of butter until brown, then drain using a piece of kitchen paper.

# ŒUFS EN MEURETTE

When the sauce has reduced by half, take the pan off the heat. Remove the bones and vegetables, then whisk in the creamed butter gradually, a knob at a time, until the mixture becomes smooth. Sieve this sauce, check the seasoning, then add the bacon and mushrooms, and keep warm.

Pour 3/4 litre of red wine into a deep frying pan, add salt and pepper and bring to the boil.

Meanwhile, toast six slices of bread (without crusts), then rub them with garlic and keep them warm on plates.

When the wine has come to the boil, break and add the eggs with a brisk movement, leave them to cook for 3 to 4 minutes, then drain them.

Arrange two eggs on each slice of bread, cover with piping hot sauce and serve immediately.

LE RÉCAMIER

★ DOMAINE DE LA FERTÉ-GIVRY 1993 - Antonin Rodet
*A light and easy wine which will pleasantly accompany this dish without overwhelming it.*

★★ SAINT ROMAIN 1990 - Alain Gras
*Fine, delicate. Suits the egg and the subtlety of the recipe.*

# CASSOLETTE D'ESCARGOTS

## SNAIL CASSOLETTE

Preparation **45 min** Cooking time **2 hrs** Equipment **large saucepan, casserole**

SERVES 6

1.5 kg live snails
2 carrots
2 large onions
3 cloves
2 pinches of nutmeg
1 large bouquet garni
(thyme, bay leaf, celery, parsley)
salt and pepper
300 g button mushrooms
300 g oyster mushrooms, Horn of Plenty or field mushrooms
300 g Cantharellus infundibuliformis, Wood Hedgehog mushrooms or Wood Blewits
300 g chanterelles
300 g Lactarius sanguifluus
or Lactarius deliciosus
(basically, five types of mushroom must be used; mushrooms from fields, woods and hedge-rows)
150 g butter
2 crushed cloves of garlic
1 stem of chopped parsley

Boil the snails for 3 minutes, then drain well.

Next, remove them from their shells taking care to cut off the end of the spiral (soft, black part). Put the snails into the casserole, add 2 litres of water, salt and pepper, and the herbs wrapped in a piece of muslin, (together with roughly chopped carrots, whole onions and the bouquet garni).

Cook over a very low heat for 2 hours.

Meanwhile, peel and wash the mushrooms, then fry in a little oil until any water has completely evaporated. Drain using a sieve.

Just before serving, put the drained snails and the mushrooms into a frying pan with the butter over a high heat. Fry until the mushrooms are slightly brown, then add the garlic and chopped parsley.

Serve in a casserole.

☆☆☆ CHÂTEAU DE RULLY 1986 - Antonin Rodet

*An excellent classic, very vegetal, which has a taste of toasted bread. Perfect for the mushrooms.*

# ESCARGOTS À LA BOURGUIGNONNE

## BURGUNDY-STYLE SNAILS

Preparation **1 hr** Cooking time **3 hrs** Equipment **Large saucepan and snail-dishes**

SERVES 6

6 dozen snails
SNAIL BUTTER :
250 g butter
2 finely chopped shallots
2 cloves of garlic (grated)
1 bunch of finely chopped parsley
1 small bunch of finely chopped chervil
1 teaspoon salt
1/2 teaspoon freshly ground pepper
1 pinch of allspice
COURT-BOUILLON :
1 stick of celery
2 onions
1 carrot
1 bouquet garni of thyme
1 glass of dry white wine
salt
freshly ground pepper

Sweat the snails in 3 dessertspoons of cooking salt for 2 hours, then wash in cold water until they are no longer sticky.

Next, put snails into 5 litres of boiling water, bring back to the boil and cook for 5 minutes. Drain them immediately and run under cold water.

Empty the shells, remove any slime and the black tails.

Then prepare a very spicy court-bouillon and add the snails so that they are well covered by the liquid. Simmer for 3 hours. Leave to cool in the court-bouillon.

Meanwhile, prepare the snail butter by mixing all the ingredients thoroughly and put it to one side.

Also, clean the shells carefully and drain.

Before putting the snails back into their shells, put a knob of snail butter into each shell, then the flesh followed by more of the butter. Keep them in a cool place for 24 hours so that the butter mixture can flavour the snails.

Warm them in the oven without letting the butter boil. Serve immediately.

*For this recipe, snails which are hibernating are better than active snails*

☆☆ PULIGNY MONTRACHET 1992 - 1er Cru - Clos de la Mouchère (Volnay) - J. Boillot
*A powerful wine whose acidity enhances the flavours of this recipe. A wine for keeping which will be even better in a few years time.*

# GOUGÈRES

Preparation **20 min** Cooking time **20 min** Equipment **greased baking tray**

SERVES 6

| | |
|---|---|
| 1/4 l water | 4 eggs + 1 egg yolk to glaze |
| 100 g butter | 100 g Gruyère cheese |
| 150 g flour | 1 pinch of salt |

Grate the cheese, put it aside.

Pour the water into a thick-based saucepan, add the butter and the pinch of salt.

Bring to the boil, take the pan off the heat and add the flour. Mix well.

Dry out the mixture over the heat by beating hard with a wooden spatula, until it comes away from the sides of the pan.

Remove from the heat and add the eggs one by one beating constantly, and then add the grated cheese.

Using a dessertspoon, put egg-shaped mounds of mixture onto the greased baking tray.

Glaze the tops of the gougeres with egg yolk and bake in a preheated moderate oven (mark 6 / 180°C) for about 20 minutes.

*This dish is the most traditional appetizer in Burgundy to bring out the best of the wine*

*Gougeres are also made in a ring shape.*

☆ BOURGOGNE ALIGOTÉ DE BOUZERON 1992 A. & P de Villaine

*An expressive smell, elegant, without acidity, this wine is perfect for an aperitif.*

# GÂTEAU SALÉ DE DÔLE

## SAVOURY DOLE CAKE

Preparation **25 min** Cooking time **1 hr** Equipment **deep sandwich tin**

SERVES 4

| | |
|---|---|
| 6 eggs | 200 g of grated Comté cheese |
| 1 dessertspoon oil | 1 Morteau sausage |
| 1 glass of white Macon wine | salt |
| 250 g flour | freshly ground pepper |
| 1 sachet of baking powder | butter for greasing the tin |

Sieve the flour, add the baking powder, mix well, put to one side.

Break the eggs into a large bowl, add the oil and wine, mix well using a wooden spatula, then sprinkle over the flour and the grated cheese, salt and pepper and stir well. Beat until smooth.

Meanwhile, cut the sausage into cubes, add to the mixture and beat thoroughly with the spatula.

Grease the tin well and add the mixture (halfway up the tin).

Bake the cake in a preheated moderate oven (mark 6 / 180°C), for 1 hour, until a skewer comes out clean when inserted.

Serve hot as a starter with a salad using ingredients in season.

*This savoury cake can also be eaten cold and can be kept for 4 to 5 days in a cool place.*

☆ Pouilly Fuissé - Cuvée vieilles vignes 1993 - Roger Lassarat
*Slightly smoky, this wine goes with Morteau sausage perfectly and livens up the whole dish...*

# LE JAMBON PERSILLÉ

## PARSLEYED HAM

Preparation **20 min** De-salting **between 6 and 24 h** depending on how heavily salted
Cooking time **1/4 hr per pound** Equipment **large casserole and terrine dish**

SERVES 6

1 Prague ham
1 shin of veal
4 l water
1 bottle of young dry white Burgundy wine
4 carrots sliced longwise
4 onions (2 stuck with cloves)
1 stick of celery
1 sprig of rosemary
2 sage leaves
12 peppercorns
1 pinch of curry powder
1 bouquet garni
no salt

PARSLEY MIXTURE
4 finely chopped shallots
2 cloves of garlic (crushed in a garlic press)
4 dessertspoons parsley
4 dessertspoons chervil
1 dessertspoon tarragon
3 dessertspoons butter

Cut the ham into 5 large pieces keeping the bones, then place in the casserole, cover with cold water and bring slowly to a simmer.

Next, drain the ham and taste it. If the meat is still too salty, repeat the blanching operation, this time covering the ham with warm water to avoid toughening the meat, then drain.

Then, pour 4 litres of water and the wine into the casserole, add the carrots, onions, stick of celery, rosemary, sage leaves and peppercorns, the bouquet garni and the pinch of curry powder.

Bring to the boil and cook for 25 minutes.

Meanwhile, remove the rind from the ham, then put the ham into the stock with the rind, bones, and the shin of veal (including the bone).

Simmer for 2 hours. The ham should be tender when pressed with a spoon and the bone should come away in the hand when still hot.

Meanwhile, prepare the parsley mixture : sweat the parsley, chervil and tarragon in a pan with butter for 3 minutes.

Next, place the sweated herbs in a bowl with the garlic and the shallots, mix thoroughly and put aside.

Now take all the ingredients out of the stock, which should be strained and clarified. Add 1 decilitre of brandy (flambéd), a glass of good red port and a few leaves of gelatine, mix well and check seasoning.

Test the consistency of the jelly by putting 2 or 3 spoonfuls of stock into the refrigerator in a saucer.

If the consistency is not right, add some gelatine which has been softened under cold water and drained.

ASSEMBLING THE TERRINE

First, place a layer of finely chopped rind and shin of veal meat in the base of the terrine dish.

Then, roughly mash the ham with a fork and add to the base layer. Next, fill the terrine with alternate layers of ham and parsley mixture.

Finish with another layer of chopped rind and veal. Press down well, then pour over the almost cold jelly. Keep in the refrigerator for 2 days.

To take out of the mould easily, soak the bottom of the terrine in boiling water for 1 to 2 minutes.

Serve the ham as a starter, cut into slices.

*Parsleyed ham or Easter ham is a typical and traditional Burgundy recipe.*

☆ BOURGOGNE ALIGOTÉ DE BOUZERON 1992 - A. et P. de Villaine

*The expressive smell and lack of acidity of this elegant wine suit the aperitif or starter stage of the meal very well.*

☆☆ CHÂTEAU DE RULLY 1992 - Antonin Rodet

*A great Burgundy classic which traditionally accompanies parsleyed ham.*

# GRATIN DE ROSÉS DES PRÉS

## WILD MUSHROOM GRATIN

Preparation **25 min** Cooking time **25 min** Equipment **earthenware dish** (or other heat-resistant dish)

SERVES 4

| | |
|---|---|
| 850 g field mushrooms | 1 bunch of chopped parsley |
| 2 dl Pouilly Fuissé wine | 1 pinch of grated nutmeg |
| 1 clove of garlic | 70 g of grated Gruyère cheese |
| juice of a lemon | 35 g butter |
| 1 tomato | salt, freshly ground pepper |

Cut off the earthy base of the mushrooms, wash and dry them and cut into halves or quarters (depending on the size). Put them into a pan with the tomato cut into quarters, the crushed clove of garlic, lemon juice and the white wine.

Add salt and pepper, cook over a high heat for 7 minutes.

Leave to cool for a few minutes, then drain and put the mushrooms into the Magimix food processor with a knife fitted and blend roughly.

Next, put the mushrooms back into the pan, add the chopped parsley and half of the grated cheese. Mix carefully, check the seasoning which should be quite spicy.

Grease the dish using half of the butter and add the mixture. Sprinkle with nutmeg and the rest of the Gruyère, then dot with butter.

Bake in a preheated hot oven (mark 6 / 180°C) for 25 minutes until golden. Serve.

*Generally, in my family, this dish is served with a roast leg of lamb.*

☆☆ BEAUNE CLOS DES MOUCHES 1992 - Chanson Père et Fils

*A pleasant wine which has finesse and roundness. Both fruity and floral, it enhances the flavour of the mushrooms.*

# GRENOUILLES FRITES

## FRIED FROGS LEGS

Preparation **10 min** Cooking time **15 min** Equipment **frying pan**

SERVES 4

24 frogs legs (with the skin removed)
1/2 l milk
2 eggs
100 g flour
salt
freshly ground pepper
Persillade (a mixture of finely chopped parsley with crushed garlic)
rapeseed oil for frying

Pour the milk into a bowl, add salt and pepper. Dip the frogs legs first into the milk, then into the beaten egg.

Next, roll them in flour and fry them in very hot oil until well cooked.

Meanwhile, prepare the parsley and garlic mixture.

When cooked, drain the frogs legs on a piece of kitchen paper and serve on a hot dish sprinkled with the persillade.

The garlic is optional, depending on personal tastes. In my family, we leave it out.

*When we were children, my cousins and I often went fishing for frogs, armed only with a rod and a red rag.*

☆ CHABLIS GRAND CRU 1990 - Le Vaudésir - Domaine Long-Depaquit - A. Bichot
*A strength which suits the frog flesh well.*

☆☆ CHÂTEAU DE CHAMIRAY 1990 - Antonin Rodet
*A good Mercurey whose lovely smell and freshness harmonize well with this dish.*

# PÂTÉ EN CROÛTE

Preparation **25 min and 15 min** the day before Cooking time **1 hr** Equipment **paté dish**

SERVES 8

300 g loin of veal
300 g loin of pork
500 g collar of pork
100 g foie gras
6 pieces of truffle
1 glass white Burgundy
1 glass cognac
500 g shortcrust pastry
3 eggs
2 bards of fat
salt
freshly ground pepper
a good pinch of allspice
1/2 l jelly (1 sachet of Madeira jelly)

Cut the loin of veal and pork into small cubes. Place in a large basin, sprinkle with white wine and cognac. Add salt, pepper and allspice. Mix well, leave to marinate overnight.

Next day, prepare shortcrust pastry : place sieved flour on a pastry board, add a good pinch of salt. Make a well in the centre, add 2 eggs. Knead the dough with 300 g softened butter. Put aside in a cool place.

Mince the collar of pork in a Magimix fitted with a knife. Add to the marinade. Chop the foie gras into small dice and add to the meat mixture. Stir carefully, taste and check seasoning.

Roll out the pastry and line the dish (keeping enough pastry for a lid). Place a bard on the base, and add half of the mixture. Cover with the other bard and then the remaining meat mixture. Seal the lid carefully and make two small air holes (using paper horns as funnels). Brush with beaten egg. Cook in a preheated hot oven (fan-assisted mark 9 / 250°C) for 1 hour. Leave to cool overnight.

Prepare the jelly. When it is cool but still liquid, pour into the paté through the holes. Place in the refrigerator for 24 hours before eating.

JEAN DUCLOUX

# MATEFAIM AUX FINES HERBES

## SOUFFLÉ OMELETTE WITH FINES HERBES

Preparation **20 min** Cooking time **15 min** Equipment **large, deep frying pan**

SERVES 5/6

2 eggs
200 g flour
approx. 2 dl milk (according to consistency)
1 bunch of chopped parsley
1 bunch of chopped chervil
1 bunch of chopped chives
2 dessertspoons butter
salt
freshly ground pepper

Whisk 2 egg yolks by hand in a basin, then add the flour gradually, mix well and pour in the milk while stirring constantly to obtain a batter.

Add the chopped herbs, salt and pepper and mix carefully. Next, beat the egg whites until they are in firm peaks and mix gently into the batter.

Then, melt a dessertspoon of butter in the frying pan and pour in the mixture.

Shake the pan to stop the batter sticking, and lower the heat, cover and leave to rest for 5 minutes.

Turn the omelette over and cook it for 5 minutes on the other side using the rest of the butter.

Serve hot as a starter.

The “ Matefaim ” is good served with thin slices (not too thin!) of smoked ham, which are even better if you warm them in the pan first.

*Can also be served with a salad as a light meal.*

# PÂTÉ DE TÊTE DE MARCASSIN

## YOUNG BOAR'S HEAD PATÉ

Preparation **1 hr** Soaking **6 hrs** Cooking time **3 hrs** Equipment **2.4 l oval paté dish**

SERVES 10

a young boar's head
one and a half pig heads
2 pork tongues
3 onions, 5 cloves
2 carrots
2 leeks
3 sticks of celery
1 head of garlic
1 bunch of parsley
1 bouquet garni
salt, freshly ground pepper
3 pinches paprika

Soak the heads and tongues in salted water for 6 hours.

Peel the onions, leeks, carrots and celery sticks, place in a large saucepan of salted water with the bouquet garni. Add heads and tongues. Cook for 3 hours until the meat comes away from the bones. Leave to cool.

Drain the heads, putting aside the stock. Separate the meat and cut up roughly with the tongues. Chop garlic and parsley. Add this mixture to 2 litres of the stock with 3 good pinches of paprika. Stir well, taste and check seasoning. Add the chopped meat. Mix thoroughly and place in the terrine dish. Cover with some stock. Place the terrines in the refrigerator for 12 hours.

Reduce the remaining stock, check seasoning and add a little chopped parsley, then place in the refrigerator.

Serve slices of paté with chopped jelly.

LE RÉCAMIER

★ BOURGOGNE ALIGOTE DE BOUZERON 1992 - A. et P de Villaine

★ CHÂTEAU DE MERCEY 1990 - Mercurey 1er Sazenay

★★★ CHAMBOLLE - MUSIGNY 1991 - Domaine J. Prieur

# SALADE DE TRUFFES FRAÎCHES

## FRESH TRUFFLE SALAD

Preparation **20 min** | No cooking | Equipment **salad bowl**

SERVES 4

| | |
|---|---|
| 6 truffles (50 g each) | 1 lemon |
| 2 hard-boiled eggs | 200 g lamb's lettuce |
| 6 Limousin walnuts | salt |
| 2 dessertspoons olive oil | freshly ground white pepper |

Pick over and wash the lamb's lettuce, drain and put it aside.

Take succulent fresh truffles, cut them into strips, add salt and pepper and put them into the salad bowl.

Chop the eggs and the walnuts, add the olive oil and a dash of lemon, and mix carefully with the truffles in the salad bowl.

Arrange the mixture on a serving dish, on a bed of lamb's lettuce placed in a ring to look like petals of a flower, then sprinkle with the grated egg yolks as a garnish.

LE RÉCAMIER

☆☆☆ PULIGNY MONTRACHET 1992 - Les Combettes - Domaine J. Prieur
*Powerful and lively wine which enhances the aromas of the truffle admirably.*

☆☆☆ MONTRACHET 1990 - Domaine J. Prieur
*A delicate, elegant and full-bodied wine for an elegant starter with powerful flavours.*

# OMELETTE MORVANDELLE

## MORVANDELLE OMELETTE

Preparation **5 min** Cooking time **4 min** Equipment **large frying pan**

SERVES 4

1 large, thick slice of raw ham (e.g Parma) with its fat
9 eggs
20 g butter
salt
freshly ground pepper

Remove the rind (if there is any) from the ham, leaving the fat, then cut the slice into 4 pieces.

Next, beat the eggs in a small basin, add little salt (as the ham is already salted) and pepper.

Meanwhile, melt the butter in the frying pan, then fry the pieces of ham for 1 minute on each side.

Next, pour over the eggs, making sure that some egg goes under the slices of ham, and cover the pan.

As soon as the eggs have set, still slightly runny, slide the omelette onto a hot serving dish, cut it into 4, and serve.

☆☆☆ MEURSAULT CHARMES 1989 - Domaine des Comtes Lafon
*An excellent wine which will add its noble character to this simple dish.*

# ŒUFS À LA MOUTARDE

## EGGS COOKED IN MUSTARD

Preparation **20 min** Cooking time **10 min** Equipment **ovenproof earthenware dish**

**SERVES 6**

| | |
|---|---|
| 6 eggs | 1 bunch of chopped tarragon |
| 30 g butter | 2 dessertspoons of single cream |
| 1 dessertspoon mustard | a dash of vinegar |
| 1 chopped shallot | salt |
| 1 bunch of chopped parsley | freshly ground pepper |
| 1 bunch of chopped chervil | |

Hard-boil the eggs for 10 minutes in boiling water, then run under cold water.

Remove the shells, cut into half longwise, remove the yolks and put the whites to one side.

Mash the yolks in a basin, add the mustard, cream, herbs and chopped shallot, mix well, add salt and pepper and check the seasoning if necessary.

Fill the egg whites with the herb mixture, arrange them on the dish, and sprinkle with the melted butter and vinegar.

Cook in a preheated hot oven (mark 7 / 200°C) for 10 minutes.

Serve as a starter.

# SOUFFLÉ DE FOIES DE VOLAILLE

## CHICKEN LIVER SOUFFLÉ

Preparation **30 min** Cooking time **1 hr 15 min** Equipment **soufflé tin**

SERVES 6

500 g poultry livers (chicken, duck, rabbit, etc...)
1 clove of garlic
1 small bunch of chopped parsley
5 cl fresh cream
2 eggs
35 g flour
30 g butter
1 dl milk
salt
freshly ground pepper
tomato sauce

Blend the liver with the garlic and parsley, add the cream, stir well, then add the egg yolks one by one beating carefully. Put this mixture aside.

Next, prepare a thick bechamel sauce with the milk, flour and butter. Add salt and pepper. Stir in the liver mousse and mix well.

Then beat the egg whites to firm peaks and fold them gently into the mixture.

Grease the tin well, pour in the mixture and cook in a moderate oven (mark 5 / 160°C) for about 1 hour 15 minutes.

Leave to cool for a few minutes after taking it out of the oven, before removing from the soufflé tin. Serve as a starter with a tomato sauce.

☆☆ LADOIX 1991 - Côte de Beaune - Chevalier Père et Fils
*A very floral wine. At the same time both rich and fresh. Its opulence suits this soufflé well.*

# TERRINE DE CHEVREUIL

## VENISON TERRINE

Preparation **40 min** Cooking time **1 hr 50 min** Equipment **oval terrine dish ovenproof**

SERVES 6

750 g fillet of venison
250 g loin of pork
200 g bacon
2 liqueur glasses of Burgundy marc
1 dl of white Burgundy wine
2 eggs
2 finely chopped shallots
1 dessertspoon of chopped parsley
1 teaspoon of allspice
salt (15 g per kg of meat)
freshly ground pepper
1 sachet of aspic jelly
1 large caul or thin slices of pork fat
1 dessertspoon of flour and some water to seal the terrine

Prepare the aspic jelly.

Meanwhile, cut the venison into two pieces, cut one into 6 attractive slices, sprinkle them with marc and put aside. Cut all the other meat into pieces and blend, then add 1/2 glass of warm aspic.

After that, put the eggs into an earthenware basin, add the chopped shallots, parsley, salt and pepper, pour over the wine and remaining marc, whisk well.

Next, beat in the meat mixture gradually, checking the seasoning which should be quite spicy. Rinse the caul in cold water, dry it carefully and use to line the terrine, leaving it to overlap (otherwise use thin slices of pork fat).

Place a thick layer of the meat mixture at the bottom, then cover with 3 of the venison fillets, press down well and repeat the layers, finshing with a layer of meat mixture Press down well. Fold over the caul or fat, put on the lid and seal the edges with flour and water. Cook in a preheated fan oven for 1 hour 50 minutes (mark 6-7 /190°C). Check from time to time.

When the terrine is cooked, carefully remove the flour seal and the lid, and remove the caul or fat on the top. Leave the terrine to cool completely, then remove any fat and add the remaining aspic jelly. Keep in the refrigerator for at least 48 hours, before eating this terrine with gherkins and small onions.

*If you do not have a fan oven, you need to cook the terrine in a bain-marie (you can use a shallow baking tin half-filled with water).*

☆ FAIVELEY 1993 - Hautes Côtes de Nuits «Dames Huguettes»
*A delicate wine which is in harmony with the finesse of the terrine.*

☆ MARSANNAY 1993 - Huguenot Père et Fils
*A light and floral wine which is ideal for first courses or as an aperitif.*

# Vegetables

*Vegetables are robust in Burgundy...*
*From the flavour of baby vegetables in Spring*
*to winter cabbages, through dried vegetables,*
*they take account of seasonal changes, that farming*
*helps along a little with early crops, like asparagus*
*or Chinese artichokes which are once more*
*becoming available.*

*Everyday cuisine is also included,*
*and you will discover great classics*
*such as potato soufflé, potato au gratin,*
*leeks in a red wine sauce, or kidney beans*
*in Burgundy wine.*

# CHOU VERT BRAISÉ

## BRAISED GREEN CABBAGE

Preparation **20 min** Cooking time **1 hr 30 min** Equipment **casserole**

SERVES 4

1 green cabbage (about 1 kg)
50 g diced onions
50 g diced carrots
50 g smoked bacon
1 bouquet garni
1/2 l chicken stock
60 g butter
salt
freshly ground pepper

Remove and discard the outer leaves of the cabbage. Separate the rest into individual leaves, and blanch them in lightly salted boiling water for two minutes. Add cold water, then drain the leaves carefully. Cut each leaf into 2 or 3 according to their size.

Dice the bacon.

Melt 30 g butter in the casserole, add the bacon, onions and carrots, put on the lid and leave to cook for two minutes.

Add the cabbage leaves, the bouquet garni, then pour in the chicken stock, and season with salt and pepper.

Bake in a preheated moderate oven (mark 6 /180°C) for 1 hour 30.

Check the cooking and stir occasionally.

When cooked, take the casserole out of the oven, and bring to the boil over a reasonably high heat to evaporate the juice.

Taste and check the seasoning, add the rest of the butter.

Serve on a hot dish.

☆ BOURGOGNE 1992 - Les Champlains - Simon Bize et Fils

# MATELOTE DE POIREAUX

## LEEKS IN A WINE SAUCE

Preparation **15 min** Cooking time **15 min** Equipment **casserole and small frying pan**

SERVES 4

| | |
|---|---|
| 16 leeks | 1 dessertspoon flour |
| a dash of vinegar | 1/4 l ordinary red Burgundy |
| a handful of cooking salt | 1 bouquet garni |
| SAUCE | salt |
| 1 large onion | freshly ground pepper |
| 30 g butter | 16 croutons |

Peel the leeks, leave whole and cook in salted boiling water for 15 minutes. Leave to drain sprinkled with a dash of vinegar.

Meanwhile, prepare the sauce :

Peel the onion, chop and fry in the small frying pan with the butter, then sprinkle with the flour, shake briskly and add the wine. Mix well, add the bouquet garni, leave to reduce, add salt and pepper, and taste to check seasoning.

Arrange the leeks on a hot serving dish, surrounded by freshly toasted croutons.

Strain the sauce and pour over the leeks.

Serve immediately.

# MOUSSE DE CAROTTES EN CHARLOTTE

## CARROT MOUSSE CHARLOTTE

Preparation **20 min** Cooking time **50 min** Equipment **charlotte tin**

SERVES 6

750 g carrots
a small handful of cooking salt
60 g butter
2 dessertspoons flour
2 dl milk
4 eggs
1 level teaspoon of grated nutmeg
1 teaspoon of salt
1 teaspoon of freshly ground pepper
butter to grease the tin

Peel the carrots, chop them (with the knife fitted in the food processor), then blanch for 15 minutes in a saucepan of salted boiling water.

Next, drain and dry them quickly in a frying pan with 25 g of butter.

Blend the carrots with your Magimix to a smooth purée, put aside.

Meanwhile, melt 35 g butter in a saucepan, sprinkle with flour, stir briskly then add the milk gradually, stirring continually. Leave to thicken, add salt, pepper and nutmeg, then pour the bechamel sauce into a basin. Add the egg yolks one by one, stir well. Next, mix in the carrot purée, and blend thoroughly. Put the mixture aside.

Whisk the egg whites into firm peaks and fold carefully into the carrot mixture.

Check the seasoning.

Grease the tin well, and fill with the mixture.

Cook in a preheated moderate oven (fan oven mark 6 / 180°C) for 50 minutes.

Check from time to time. When cooked, leave to rest for 10 minutes before removing from the tin.

*Serve hot as a starter or to accompany roast veal.*

# OIGNONS FARCIS

## STUFFED ONIONS

Preparation **40 min** Cooking time **40 min** Equipment **earthenware dish**

SERVES 6

| | |
|---|---|
| 6 large sweet onions | 40 g butter |
| Stuffing : | 1/4 l veal stock |
| 125 g sausagemeat | salt |
| 125 g shoulder of veal | freshly ground pepper |
| 60 g mushrooms | bread-crumbs |

Peel the onions, blanch them for 10 minutes in boiling water, and then drain.

Cut out a lid from each onion three-quarters from the bottom. Hollow them out using a spoon without damaging the bases. Put aside.

Next, chop the discarded onion, then into a frying pan with some butter.

Meanwhile, cut off the ends of the mushroom stalks, rinse, and wipe dry.

Chop the mushrooms with the meat, then put mix with the fried onions. Add some stock, salt and pepper. Blend the stuffing well and check the seasoning which should be spicy.

Fill the onions, arrange them in a dish and sprinkle with bread-crumbs.

Bake until golden in a preheated moderate oven (mark 6 / 180°C) for 30 minutes.

During the cooking, sprinkle with the remaining stock.

☆☆☆ MÂCON CLESSÉ 1987 - Domaine de Bongran - Cuvée spéciale Levrouté - Jean Thévenet

*A late harvested wine, with a flavour reminiscent of truffles, whose softness matches the onion perfectly.*

★★★★ Musigny 1989 - Domaine J. Prieur

*A very great wine, delicate and full of breeding, to glorify this dish.*

# HARICOTS ROUGES AU VIN

## KIDNEY BEANS COOKED IN WINE

Preparation **15 min** Cooking time **45 min** Equipment **casserole**

SERVES 6

500 g red kidney beans
1/2 l ordinary red table wine
1/2 l water
1 bouquet garni
1 bunch of parsley
1 large onion stuck with 2 cloves
200 g of salted streaky bacon
1 dessertspoon fresh cream
freshly ground pepper

Cook the bacon (in the piece) for 10 minutes.

Meanwhile, pour the wine and water into the casserole, then add the beans, the bouquet garni, the onion stuck with cloves, and the cooked bacon. Cover and leave to cook for 45 minutes.

When the beans are cooked (check the cooking), remove the ingredients, separating the bacon, and keeping it in a warm place to be served later.

Then add the cream and pepper. Check the seasoning, serve with the bacon cut into pieces.

# POMMES DE TERRE EN GRATIN

## POTATOES AU GRATIN

Preparation **25 min** Cooking time **40 min** Equipment **earthenware dish**

Serves 6

| | |
|---|---|
| 1 kg potatoes (Belle de Fontenay variety) | 1 teaspoon of rubbed thyme |
| 250 g onions | 2 bay leaves |
| 60 g butter | salt |
| 50 cl of a good red Burgundy wine | frasly ground pepper |

Peel and chop the onions.

Cook them in a deep frying pan with some of the butter over a low heat, stirring several times.

After 10 minutes, add half of the wine, leave to cook, stirring occasionally, until the onions become brown and caramelized and the wine evaporates. Keep in a warm place.

Meanwhile, peel the potatoes, slice thinly and dry in a tea-towel. Sprinkle with a mixture of the rubbed thyme, bay leaves, salt and pepper, put aside.

Grease the tin well and place a layer of potatoes then a layer of onions, sprinkle with the herb mixture, and repeat the layers, finishing with the rest of the wine.

Bake in a preheated hot oven (mark 7 /200°C) for 35 to 40 minutes.

Serve with a fresh, crisp endive salad.

*This recipe was a speciality of my cousins from Cluny.*

# SOUFFLÉ DE POMMES DE TERRE

## POTATO SOUFFLÉ

Preparation **25 min** Cooking time **50 min** (approx) Equipment **gratin dish**

SERVES 6/8

| | |
|---|---|
| 1 kg potatoes | a pinch of grated nutmeg |
| 10 cl fresh cream | salt |
| 50 g butter | freshly ground pepper |
| 5 eggs | |

Peel the potatoes, and boil for 20 to 25 minutes. Drain and blend to obtain a smooth purée.

Thin the purée with the cream and 30 g of butter, add salt, pepper and nutmeg. Mix thoroughly, then leave to cool.

Next, add the eggs one by one while stirring constantly, taste and add seasoning if necessary. Spread the purée in the gratin dish and dot with the remaining butter.

Cook in a preheated hot oven (fan oven mark 7 / 200°C) for 30 minutes until golden brown and serve immediately.

☆☆☆ MEURSAULT CHARMES 1989 - Domaine des Comtes Lafon

*Superb wine of great maturity which will render this simple dish sublime. It should be noted that this soufflé will be all the more appreciated if it is accompanied by escalopes of foie gras.*

# Meat

*The tradition of meat from Saône-et-Loire comes from the Middle Ages.*

*Discover here all the flavours of Burgundy cuisine, past and present...*

*The Charolais race still gives the beef which is held in the highest esteem. Today, it is the best bovine race in France and it is eaten in many dishes. Next, the Charollais sheep, giving the best lamb (which differs from the beef by adding an extra 'l'). Finally, Burgundy Potée, which cannot be overlooked, being prepared in so many households.*

# ANDOUILLE AUX HARICOTS

## ANDOUILLE WITH BEANS

Preparation **20 min** Cooking time **3 1/2 hrs** Equipment **casserole**

SERVES 6

| | |
|---|---|
| 1 large andouille<br>(a sausage made of chitterlings)<br>500 g of haricot beans (dried)<br>2 carrots<br>2 medium-sized onions | 2 cloves<br>1 bouquet garni<br>1 dl Aligoté (a Burgundy grape) white wine<br>salt<br>freshly ground pepper |

Pour 2 litres of water into the casserole, add the andouille, bring to the boil and cook for 2 hours.

Meanwhile, peel the carrots and cut into slices. Peel the onions and push one clove into each, and put into a saucepan of cold water with the beans. Add the bouquet garni, salt and pepper. When the beans are half-cooked, add the white wine, bring back to the boil and cook for 1 hour.

Add the andouille and leave to simmer until completely cooked.

Remove the onions and the bouquet garni, check seasoning and serve on a hot dish.

☆ CHARDONNAY DE VIEILLES VIGNES 1993 - Bourgogne Antonin Rodet
*The freshness of this wine brings out the flavour of the sausage wonderfully, and makes the beans lighter.*

☆☆ MEURSAULT 1990 - Clos de Mazeray - Domaine J. Prieur
*A perfect marriage with the softness of the beans.*

# AIGUILLETTE DE BŒUF MODE EN GELÉE

## AIGUILLETTE OF BEEF COOKED IN JELLY

Preparation **40 min** Cooking time **3 hrs** Equipment **casserole and large frying pan**

SERVES 10

| | |
|---|---|
| 1 aiguillette barded with fat (2 kg) | 500 g leeks |
| 2 dessertspoons oil | 1 stick of celery |
| 4 shin of veal | 4 litres red wine |
| 500 g fresh pork rind | 5 cloves |
| 4 large onions | 1 bouquet garni |
| 3 large carrots | salt, freshly ground pepper |

Peel and wash the vegetables, put aside.

Meanwhile, heat the oil in the frying pan, add the aiguillette and seize on both sides, then remove from the pan.

Add 2 onions, cut into quarters, on a high heat for 20 to 30 minutes. They should be almost black to give the jelly a good colour.

Place the meat in the casserole with the remaining onions stuck with cloves, the leeks, carrots, stick of celery, shin of veal and pork rind as well as the fried onions.

Rinse the frying pan with a litre of wine and pour it into the casserole, add the rest of the wine, two litres of water, pepper and the bouquet garni and leave to cook for 3 hours on a moderate heat.

When a two-pronged fork can be inserted and removed easily, the meat is cooked. Remove from the heat and put the aiguillette into a large serving dish.

Strain the remaining juices, pour back into the casserole and leave to reduce over a low heat for another hour. Pour the sauce over the aiguillette, leave to cool and place in the refrigerator for 24 hours.

After this time, turn out and cut into thin slices.

LE RÉCAMIER

☆ CHABLIS GRAND CRU - LE VAUDÉSIR 1990 - Domaine Long Depaquit - A. Bichot
*This white with quite a deep taste has the smell of a red, and is perfectly suited to this dish.*

# CHATEAUBRIAND RÉCAMIER

Preparation **30 min** Cooking time **according to taste for the meat**
Equipment **2 (non-stick) 12 cm frying pans, deep frying pan**

SERVES 6

6 chateaubriands (best fillet) (200 g each)
12 large Charlotte potatoes
(firm flesh with a lot of starch)
DUXELLE
500 g button mushrooms
2 finely chopped shallots
150 g butter
salt
10 g crushed green peppercorns
Burgundy sauce (see Eggs in a wine sauce recipe, same quantity)

Prepare the sauce. This can be done the day before.

Clean the mushrooms, cut into pieces. Cook with a little oil in the deep frying pan until the water starts to come out of the mushrooms. Drain. Place the butter and shallots in the deep frying pan, add the mushrooms. Leave to fry until the mushroom juice has completely evaporated. Chop the mixture, add the lightly crushed peppercorns and put aside. Add this mixture (duxelle) to the red wine sauce and keep hot in a bain-marie or double boiler.

Using a 1 mm vegetable grater or mandoline, grate the potatoes finely. (Note : do not wash grated potatoes, or the starch will form a sticky lump when cooked) Add salt and pepper. Place a knob of butter and a little oil in a frying pan, leave to heat. Add the potatoes, to form an even layer, about one centimetre thick.

Cook until golden brown on both sides.

Meanwhile, cook the chateaubriands, either on the grill or in the frying pan according to personal taste. Drain the potato cake.

Serve on individual plates, placing the potatoes first, the chateaubriand on top. Coat with sauce.

★★ SAVIGNY LES BEAUNE 1990 - Les Vergelesses - J. Boillot et Fils
*This very fine wine suits the refinement of this dish, which it accompanies with elegance.*

★★ CHÂTEAU DE CHAMIREY 1985 - Antonin Rodet
*A wine with a definite personality, which enhances the flavour of the dish well.*

★★★ GEVREY CHAMBERTIN 1990 - Comtes aux Moines - Louis Jadot
*A superb robe, a good aroma, all the elegance of Gevrey Chambertin. Suits the power of the beef and the structure of the recipe to perfection.*

# CÔTES D'AGNEAU CHAMPVALLON

## CHAMPVALLON LAMB CHOPS

Preparation **25 min** Cooking time **20 min** Equipment **cast-iron casserole**

,Serves 6

| | |
|---|---|
| 8 lamb chops | 1 bouquet garni |
| 1 dessertspoon oil | 100 g butter |
| 300 g onions | 1 generous kg potatoes |
| 3/4 litre of veal stock | (Charlotte or Spunta variety) |
| (or 2 stock cubes and 3/4 l water) | salt, freshly ground pepper |

Peel and thinly slice the onions, fry until golden with 80 g butter, put aside.

Meanwhile, peel the potatoes, slice in a food processor using the medium slicing blade, put into a saucepan with some court-bouillon, thyme and bay leaf, salt and pepper and cook for 10 minutes until there is no more liquid.

Seize the lamb chops over a high heat in a frying pan with the oil, then discard the oil and deglaze the pan with some court-bouillon.

Place a layer of potatoes in the base of the casserole, covered with the lamb chops, onions and bouquet garni. Cover with the rest of the potatoes, add the veal stock, salt and pepper. Put on the lid and cook gently for about 20 minutes.

Check the potatoes are cooked.

Serve very hot.

★★ Beaune Clos des Marconnets 1988 - Chanson Père et Fils

*This wine, with aromas typical of the year 1988, offers all the finesse of the Beaune wines. Easy to drink and seductive, it suits the tender aspect of the lamb.*

★★★★ Musigny 1989 - Domaine J. Prieur

*Delicate and full of finesse, a superb wine which will enhance the subtlety of the lamb meat.*

# CÔTE DE BŒUF CHAROLAIS AUX MORILLES

## CHAROLAIS RIBS OF BEEF WITH MOREL MUSHROOMS

Preparation **15 min** Cooking time **40 min** Equipment **roasting pan and a small, deep frying pan**

SERVES 6

1 rib of beef (1.5 kg)
a handful of cooking salt
freshly ground pepper
500 g of morel mushrooms
35 g butter

SHALLOT SAUCE
4 shallots
25 g butter
1.5 dl dry burgundy
1 dessertspoon vinegar
2 egg yolks

Remove the fat from the beef (or ask your butcher to do it), then roll it in the cooking salt and place in the roasting tin.

Put into a preheated hot oven (mark 8 /230°C)

Meanwhile, prepare the sauce :

Peel and chop the shallots, fry gently in the butter without letting them brown, sprinkle with wine, add salt and pepper. Add the vinegar and reduce liquid by half.

Next, whisk in the egg yolks. Put into a double saucepan, leave to thicken and put aside.

Pick over and clean the morel mushrooms, and fry in butter.

Serve the beef on a hot dish, covered with sauce and garnished with mushrooms.

★ DOMAINE DES HAUTES CORNIÈRES 1990 - Santenay Commes 1er Cru - Chapelle et Fils
*This structured and powerful wine, with an aroma full of expression accompanies red meats unaffectedly.*

★★★ FAIVELEY 1991- Nuits Saint-Georges 1er Cru- Les Forêts Saint-Georges
*A fiery wine, as much in aroma as in taste, wholly appropriate to a red meat.*

# ÉTUVÉE DE VEAU MARINIÈRE

## BRAISED VEAL MARINIÈRE

Preparation **25 min** Cooking time **1 hr 30 min** Equipment **casserole**

SERVES 6

1 boneless shoulder of lamb
50 g butter
2 medium onions (chopped)
1 dessertspoon flour
1/2 l red Burgundy
2 chopped shallots
1 bouquet garni
250 g mushrooms
10 cl fresh cream
salt, freshly ground pepper

Cut the meat into cubes, fry in the casserole with the butter and chopped onions. Leave to brown, then sprinkle with flour, stir briskly, add the wine and stir again. Next, add the shallots, bouquet garni, salt and pepper, cover and leave to simmer for 1 hour on a low heat.

Meanwhile, cut off the ends of the mushroom stalks, wash under cold water and pat dry. Cut into halves or quarters according to size.

When the casserole is almost cooked, add the mushrooms and cook for another fifteen minutes.

Just before serving, stir in the cream carefully, check seasoning.

Serve on a hot dish.

★★ SAINT-ROMAIN 1990 - Alain Gras
*A very subtle wine which suits this delicate and simple dish.*

# JAMBON À LA NUITONNE

## BURGUNDY-STYLE HAM

Preparation **20 min** Cooking time **25 min** Equipment **earthenware dish**

SERVES 6

| | |
|---|---|
| 4 thick slices of raw ham (e.g Parma) | 25 cl cream |
| 1 glass of dry white wine | 2 egg yolks |
| 2 dessertspoons wine vinegar | 1 pinch of nutmeg |
| 40 g butter | salt |
| 2 finely chopped shallots | freshly ground pepper |

Cut the ham into thin strips, then arrange them on the dish. Melt the butter in a deep frying pan. Brown the shallots, then add the wine and vinegar.

Reduce on a low heat to obtain 4 dessertspoons of liquid, and stir in the cream.

Heat gently, whisking constantly, and add salt, pepper and nutmeg.

Beat the egg yolks, then stir them into the mixture.

Strain and pour over the ham.

Place in a preheated low oven (fan oven mark 5 / 160°C) for 20 minutes, then brown for a few moments in a very hot oven (mark 8 - 9) without letting the dish burn.

Serve immediately.

☆ DOMAINE DE BONGRAN - Cuvée Tradition - J. Thévenet
*An elegant wine which enhances the simple flavours of the dish.*

# JAMBON EN SAUPIQUET

## HAM RAGOUT

Preparation **10 min** Cooking **10 min** Equipment **frying pan**

SERVES 6

| | |
|---|---|
| 6 slices of Morvan ham | 1 dessertspoon flour |
| 1 glass of vinegar | 1 dl Burgundy white wine |
| 6 juniper berries | 1/2 glass stock |
| 6 peppercorns | 15 cl cream |
| 3 chopped shallots | 1 bunch of fines herbes (parsley, chervil, tarragon, chives) |
| 1 sprig of tarragon | salt, freshly ground pepper |
| 70 g butter | |

Pour the vinegar into a small pan with the juniper berries and crushed peppercorns. Add the shallots and sprig of tarragon, bring to the boil and leave to reduce by half.

Meanwhile, fry the ham in butter on both sides, remove from the pan and keep on a serving dish in a warm place.

Next put the flour into the frying pan and stir briskly. Pour in the white wine and stock, mix well, leave to cook for 5 minutes over a low heat, then add the vinegar and herb mixture, and leave to cook for another 5 minutes.

Strain the sauce, pour back into the pan and add the cream, pepper (the ham is already salted) and check seasoning.

Warm without letting the mixture boil and pour over the ham.

Serve the ham sprinkled with the finely chopped fines herbes.

☆ CHABLIS GRAND CRU LES VAUDÉSIRS 1990 - Domaine Long Depaquit - Albert Bichot
*An animal strength which enhances the dish.*

# PÂTÉ CHAUD BOURGUIGNON

## HOT BURGUNDY PATÉ

Preparation **30 min** Cooking time **50 min** Equipment **earthenware dish**

SERVES 6

500 g shortcrust pastry
350 g cushion of veal
350 g belly of pork

MARINADE
1 medium onion (chopped)
2 cloves of garlic (crushed)
1 dessertspoon chopped parsley
1 liqueur glass of Burgundy marc
salt
freshly ground pepper

Prepare the shortcrust pastry and leave to rest for 2 hours.

Mix the marinade ingredients. Cut the pork and veal into large cubes, then stir well with the marinade mixture. Leave for 2 hours to absorb the flavour.

Roll out the pastry, divide in half, then line the dish with one half.

Roughly chop the meat and make balls the size of a large egg. Arrange the meat balls on the pastry then cover using the other half as a lid.

Use egg white to seal the edges, and press them together to make it look attractive. Glaze with egg yolk.

Place in a preheated moderate oven (mark 5-6 /170°C) for 50 minutes.

*This traditional dish from Lower Burgundy often used to be served at weddings.*

★★ CHÂTEAU DE CHAMIREY 1983 - Antonin Rodet
*Rich in tertiary aromas, this wines suits white meats perfectly as it does not overwhelm them.*

★★★ VOLNAY SANTENOTS DU MILIEU 1989
*A generous wine, suitable for this regional speciality to which it will lend an aristocratic quality.*

# FONDUE BOURGUIGNONNE

## BURGUNDY-STYLE FONDUE

Preparation **15 min** | Cooking time **1 hr** | Equipment **casserole**

SERVES 6

| | |
|---|---|
| 1.250 kg fillet of beef | 1 bay leaf |
| 2 l Burgundy | 3 crushed cloves of garlic |
| 2 shin of veal | 2 liqueur glasses of Burgundy marc |
| 4 cloves | salt |
| 3 sprigs of thyme | freshly ground pepper |

Seize the shin of veal in a small pan, add the cloves, crushed garlic, thyme, bay leaf, salt, pepper and wine.

Cook slowly and reduce by half, then remove the flavourings and pour the wine into the pan of a fondue set.

Meanwhile, cut the meat into cubes and arrange on a large dish.

Place the burner of the fondue set in the middle of the table, with the pan on top. Add the marc and bring to simmering point.

Each guest then takes a cube of meat and cooks it in the wine mixture to his taste.

*This traditional fondue is traditionally served with steamed potatoes which are also soaked in the wine mixture.*

★ BOURGOGNE RODET 1990 - Pinot noir de vieilles vignes
*This wine enhances this simple dish pleasantly, through its powerful character.*

# ROGNONS DE VEAU AU SANTENAY

## CALVES KIDNEYS IN SANTENAY WINE SAUCE

Preparation **1 hr 30 min** Cooking time **a few min** Equipment **saucepans and frying pans**

SERVES 6

| | |
|---|---|
| 3 carefully chosen calves kidneys | 1 head of garlic |
| 2 l Santenay red wine | table salt |
| 150 g salted bacon | cooking salt |
| 250 g button mushrooms | peppercorns |
| 60 g butter | ground pepper |
| 60 g flour | bouquet garni (parsley, tarragon, thyme, |
| 1/2 l veal stock | bay leaf, stick of celery) |
| 2 large veal bones | 100 g shallots |
| 2 carrots | 2 cl brandy |
| 3 onions | oil |

PREPARATION

Red wine sauce :

Pour 1/2 litre of water into a saucepan and add a sachet of veal stock (or a stock cube). Bring to the boil.

Meanwhile, peel, wash and chop the carrots. Peel the onions and garlic, cut into two. Prepare the bouquet garni, then clean and chop the mushrooms.

Dice the bacon into small cubes. Make a beurre manié (a smooth paste of butter creamed with flour) and put aside.

Put the two veal bones and an onion into a baking tin which has been heated in a very hot oven (mark 7-8 / 220°C), leave to brown until almost black for about 15 minutes.

Meanwhile, bring 1/4 litre of water to the boil in a saucepan, adding salt, pepper, lemon juice and a knob of butter. Add the mushrooms and cook for 15 minutes.

Next, take the veal bones and onion out of the oven, put into a casserole with the flavourings (carrots, onions, bouquet garni, head of garlic, cooking salt and crushed peppercorns), then add 1 1/2 l red wine and veal stock and cook over a high heat. Add 1/4 litre of mushroom juice and leave to cook for a little more than an hour.

Meanwhile, blanch and fry the bacon with the mushrooms, a clove of garlic and a knob of butter until golden. Remove excess fat.

When the sauce has reduced by half, remove from the heat. Remove the bones and vegetables, then mix in the beurre manié (butter mixture) a knob at a time while whisking constantly, until smooth.

Strain the sauce, check seasoning, add the mushrooms and bacon, and keep in a warm place. Remove the fat and core from the kidneys and cut into large pieces.

Heat a little oil in a frying pan, and as soon as it is hot add the kidneys. Seize well, then drain and put back in the frying pan with a knob of butter and chopped shallot.

Fry for a few seconds over a high heat, then deglaze and flambé with the brandy.

Add the red wine sauce and serve with fresh pasta and a bottle of Santenay wine.

LE RÉCAMIER

★ DOMAINE DU CHÂTEAU DE MERCEY 1990 - Santenay

*Straightforward and concentrated, this Santenay will make a vigourous contribution to this dish.*

# PÂTÉ DE VEAU DE BOURG

## BOURG VEAL PATÉ

Preparation **30 min** Cooking time **1 hr** Equipment **earthenware dish**

SERVES 6

1 kg leg of veal
150 g belly of pork
90 g breadcrumbs
1 dl warm milk
2 eggs
2 dessertspoons Burgundy marc
1 teaspoon salt
1 teaspoon freshly ground pepper
1 caul (or piece of thin pork fat)

Soak the breadcrumbs in milk.

Chop the veal and pork by hand or in your Magimix blender, make a well in the centre and add the breadcrumbs. Sprinkle with marc, salt and pepper then mix thoroughly.

Taste and check seasoning, which should be quite spicy.

Wash the caul or fat in cold water, pat dry carefully and lay on a board. Place the meat mixture onto the fat.

Form a 25 cm long sausage-shape and roll up the caul or fat ensuring that the two ends are tightly closed. Place the roll in the dish and cook in a preheated hot oven (mark 7-8 / 220°C) for 1 hour. Check the cooking and reduce oven to mark 6-7 after 45 minutes.

Serve this dish hot with freshly cooked spinach leaves arranged in a ring around it.

*Old family recipe.*

☆☆ CHARDONNAY DE VIEILLES VIGNES 1993 - Bourgogne Antonin Rodet
*Fresh and well structured, this wine, with a taste slightly reminiscent of hazelnut and long in the mouth is perfectly suited to terrines.*

☆☆ CHÂTEAU FUISSÉ 1991 - J.J. Vincent et Fils
*A delicate Pouilly fumé whose fine acidity enhances this dish perfectly.*

# PAUPIETTES AU RIS DE VEAU

## CALF SWEETBREAD PARCELS

Preparation **30 min** Cooking time **35 min** Equipment **deep frying pan**

SERVES 6

6 thin veal escalopes
1 calf sweetbread
200 g collar of pork
1 egg
1 bunch of chopped fines herbes
(parsley, tarragon, chervil, chives)
20 g butter
2 dessertspoons oil
2 chopped shallots
2 dl white Mercurey wine
25 cl cream
salt
freshly ground pepper

Soak the sweetbread in cold water for 1 hour, then place in a pan of cold salted water.

Bring to the boil, leave to cook for 10 minutes, strain and rinse immediately in cold water.

Remove skin and gristle, cut the sweetbread into 6 fairly thin slices, put aside.

Chop the pork in a blender, then add the egg, chopped herbs, salt and pepper and mix thoroughly.

Place a slice of sweetbread on each veal escalope, spread with 1/6 of the pork mixture, roll up and tie with string.

Put the parcels into the frying pan with the butter and oil. Brown on both sides. Next, discard the cooking fat and deglaze the pan with the wine, add salt, pepper, and the chopped shallots. Cover and cook for 25 minutes, checking and stirring from time to time.

Then arrange the parcels on a serving dish and keep in a warm place.

Reduce the sauce by a third, then add the cream, warm through. Strain the sauce and coat the parcels.

*Serve these parcels either with chanterelle or morel mushrooms.*

★★ CHÂTEAU DE CHAMIREY 1983 - Antonin Rodet
*Rich in tertiary aromas, this wines suits white meats perfectly as it does not overwhelm them.*

# POTÉE BOURGUIGNONNE

## BURGUNDY-STYLE STEW

Preparation **45 min** Cooking time **2 hrs 30 min** Equipment **casse-**

SERVES 7-8

| | |
|---|---|
| 1 kg salt pork | 250 g large French beans |
| 1 salted knuckle of ham | 2 cloves |
| 100 g unsalted streaky bacon | 2 onions |
| 1 green cabbage (round-headed) | 1 bouquet garni |
| 500 g carrots | salt |
| 150 g turnips | freshly ground pepper |
| 3 large leeks | 10 thin slices of farmhouse bread |
| 500 g firm potatoes (Spunta or Sirtena variety) | |

Soak the knuckle of ham overnight to remove the salt.

The next day, place the meat in the casserole and cover with water, bring to the boil.

Peel the vegetables, then add the cabbage, carrots and turnips (whole), the leeks, onions stuck with cloves and the bouquet garni, pepper but not too much salt. Cook slowly for about 2 hours.

Thirty minutes before the mixture is cooked, add the potatoes cut in halves, and the French beans.

Pour the stock over the slices of bread in a soup tureen, check seasoning.

Next serve the meat cut into slices on a large serving dish and the vegetables on another dish; the cabbage should be placed in the centre surrounded by carrots, potatoes, leeks, and French beans.

*This dish was often served on Sunday, when the family came, and was accompanied, of course, by gherkins and mustard.*

★★ BEAUNE-BRESSANDES 1988 - Chanson Père et Fils
*Quite masculine, well structured but also light and fine, this wine suits the rustic nature of the dish.*

# POITRINE DE VEAU EN MEURETTE

## BREAST OF VEAL IN A RED WINE SAUCE

Preparation **30 min** Cooking time **55 min** Equipment **deep frying pan**

SERVES 6

1.2 kg breast of veal
50 g butter
100 g bacon
2 dl red Burgundy
1 dl stock (1/2 cube)
1 dessertspoon flour
1 bouquet garni
15 small onions
salt
freshly ground pepper
100 g green olives

Cut the veal into large cubes, then fry until golden brown with the butter.

Next add the bacon, cut into dice. Sprinkle with flour, stir briskly and add the wine, salt and pepper.

Add the bouquet garni and onions, cover, simmer on a low heat for just under an hour. During cooking, add the stock and stir well.

The green olives should be added at the end of cooking.

Check seasoning, then serve on a hot dish, surrounded by the olives and small onions, vichy carrots and steamed potatoes.

★★ SAVIGNY-LES-BEAUNE 1990 - LES VERGELESSES - J. Boillot et Fils
*This wine, composed solely of Pinot Noir grapes and with great finesse, enhances the flavour of the veal perfectly.*

★★★★ CLOS VOUGEOT 1991 - Domaine J. Prieur
*Powerful aromas which highlight the flavour of the veal.*

# QUASI DE VEAU EN COCOTTE

## VEAL CASSEROLE

Preparation **35 min** Cooking time **1 hr 30 min** Equipment **casserole**

SERVES 6

| | |
|---|---|
| 750 g chump end of veal | 1/2 l white Mâcon wine |
| 6 thin slices of streaky bacon | 1 dessertspoon fresh cream |
| 5 shallots | butter to grease the casserole |
| 1 large bunch parsley | salt |
| 2 or 3 veal bones | freshly ground pepper |

Cut the veal into 6 escalopes, put aside.

Peel the shallots, chop finely with the parsley, season with salt and pepper.

Grease the casserole well, then place, in alternate layers, a slice of bacon, a slice of veal, and a layer of shallot mixture. Lay the veal bones on the top.

Add wine until halfway up the dish, cover and simmer at a low heat for 1 1/2 hours.

Just before serving, remove the bones. Check seasoning and add the cream, stir quickly and serve.

*Traditionally, this dish is served in the casserole in which it has been cooked.*

★★ BEAUNE CLOS DES MARCONNETS 1988 - Chanson
*An elegant wine with a good structure, typical of the Marconnets, whose finesse enhances the delicate aspect of the veal.*

☆☆☆☆ CORTON CHARLEMAGNE 1992 - Grand Cru - Chevalier Père et Fils
*A superb wine for keeping whose power will highlight the flavours of the veal and whose personality will add to the pleasures of the dish.*

# SAUCISSON DE LYON POMMES DE TERRE À L'HUILE

## LYON SAUSAGE WITH POTATOES IN A WARM DRESSING

Preparation **10 min** Cooking time **20 min** Equipment **deep frying pan and saucepans**

SERVES 4

2 Lyon sausages (200 g each)
2 to 3 shallots (according to size)
1 dl sherry vinegar
1 dl peanut oil
500 g firm-fleshed potatoes
(Râte or Charlotte)
salt
freshly ground pepper

Cook the sausages in the water (with no salt).

Meanwhile, cook the potatoes in their skins, in a saucepan of boiling salted water.

Peel the shallots, chop finely. Heat the vinegar in the deep frying pan on a low heat (or at the fireside of an open fire) and infuse the shallots.

Pour the oil into the warm infusion, add salt and pepper and put aside.

Drain the potatoes, peel, cut into 2 cm thick slices and put into a large bowl. Pour over the vinegar and mix carefully.

Arrange the potatoes on each plate surrounded by slices of sausage.

☆ CHÂTEAU FUISSÉ 1993 - Les Brûlés - J.J. Vincent et Fils

# SAUTÉ DE BŒUF BOURGUIGNON

## BŒUF BOURGUIGNON

Preparation **35 min** Cooking time **2 hrs 15 min** Equipment **casserole**

SERVES 8

MARINADE INGREDIENTS (cut into large chunks)
2 kg chuck steak
2 carrots
2 onions
1 bouquet garni
2 dessertspoons oil
10 black peppercorns
1 head of garlic cut into two
a few cloves

GARNISH (cut into small cubes)
3 carrots
3 onions
2 dessertspoons oil

BOURGUIGNON INGREDIENTS
400 g half-salted bacon
400 g button mushrooms

AND...
2 l red wine (Côtes-du-Rhône)
1 l veal stock (water + stock cube)
50 cl mushroom juice
120 g flour
1 bouquet garni
salt
pepper

MARINADE

Remove the fat and gristle from the meat and cut into 30 g pieces (or ask your butcher to do it for you). Put the meat into the red wine, add the carrots and the onions stuck with cloves, the bouquet garni, peppercorns, the head of garlic cut into two and the oil. Leave to marinade for at least 48 hours.

GARNISH

Peel the carrots and onions, chop into small cubes, fry gently in the oil, put aside.

BOURGUIGNON

Drain the pieces of beef, keeping the marinade juice and fry with a little oil over a high heat for 5 minutes.

Once the pieces are browned, drain and discard the cooking oil, then place in the casserole with the flavouring, mix well and put in the oven (mark 8 / 200 to 220°C).

Meanwhile, clean and remove the stalks of the mushrooms and cook in 20 g of butter for 10 minutes, then drain and put aside.

Pour the mushroom juice into the casserole, add the marinade juices and a fresh bouquet garni. Add the stock, mix well, season with salt and pepper, and leave to cook slowly for 2 hours.

Next, cut the bacon into small dice, put into 1 litre of cold water, bring to the boil and cook for 4 minutes, then drain and mix with the mushrooms. Fry this mixture, then drain off the fat and put aside.

Remove the pieces of cooked beef, one by one so that they remain whole, put them aside.

Strain the cooking juices and bring to the boil, then, mix in the beurre manié a knob at a time whisking constantly, until a satisfactory consistency is achieved.

Strain the sauce again, so that it is smoother and shinier, then add the mushrooms and bacon and pour the mixture over the pieces of meat.

Put aside and heat up just before serving.

*This recipe can be prepared in advance.*

LE RÉCAMIER

★★ CHÂTEAU DE CHAMIREY 1990 - Marquis de Jouennes d'Herville
*Supple and full-bodied. In perfect osmosis with the beef flesh.*

★★★ CLOS DES SANTENOTS 1990 - Volnay - Domaine J. Prieur
*Fine and straightforward, this cru is perfect for a generous dish.*

★★★★ CLOS VOUGEOT 1991 - Domaine J. Prieur
*A very great wine whose power is in perfect harmony with this regional speciality.*

★★★★ BONNES MARES 1989 - Joseph Drouhin
*A great wine, still young, which matches elegance with power. It balances the richness of the dish perfectly.*

# TÊTE DE VEAU À LA BOURGUIGNONNE

## BURGUNDY-STYLE CALVES HEAD

Preparation **30 min** Cooking **2 hrs 30 min** Equipment **large saucepan**

SERVES 6

1/2 calves head (blanched and rolled)
1 calves tongue
100 g bacon cut into small dice
35 g lard
2 carrots
1/2 l white Burgundy
1 large onion
1 bouquet garni
2 cloves
1 dessertspoon capers
6 gherkins
salt
freshly ground pepper

Using a clean tea-towel, dry the head and the tongue carefully. Season with salt and pepper and put aside.

Peel the vegetables, put aside.

Melt the lard in the large saucepan and fry the bacon slightly, then add the head and tongue. Brown on both sides.

Next, add the hot water and white wine (up to the top of the head), add the vegetables.

Cover, bring to the boil and cook for between 2 1/2 to 3 hours.

Skim several times during the cooking time.

Remove the head and tongue and place onto a serving dish, sprinkled with a good vinegar, keep in a cool place.

Meanwhile, reduce the stock by half, then add a dessertspoon of cornflour, leave to thicken. Strain the sauce, add the capers, stir briskly and pour over the head and tongue.

Serve with the gherkins.

☆ PERNAND-VERGELESSES 1992 - P. Dubreuil-Fontaine Père et Fils
*A very good example of a Pernand : this fine and structured wine has enough body and bouquet to be in perfect harmony with the dish and the caper sauce.*

# Poultry and Game

*Bresse poultry, chicken and poulardes*
*are prepared in ten exquisite ways ;*
*discover them simply.*

*Hare, partridge, quail,*
*pheasant and boar, not forgetting venison*
*(even it is becoming a rare and protected species)*
*are still to be found in our forests.*
*They can be accompanied naturally,*
*like our precious poultry, by marvellous*
*mushrooms growing wild.*

*From Wood Blewits to meadow mushrooms through*
*chanterelles and field mushrooms, to delicious*
*morels, let us not forget Burgundy truffles, an*
*essential ingredient of many dishes...*

# CAILLES AU RAISIN

## QUAILS WITH GRAPES

Preparation **30 min** Cooking time **30 min** Equipment **deep frying pan**

SERVES 6

| | |
|---|---|
| 6 quails (plucked and drawn) | 150 g butter |
| 6 thin pieces of pork fat | 1 teaspoon cornflour |
| 600 g white grapes | salt |
| 1 dl Burgundy marc | freshly ground pepper |
| 2 dessertspoons oil | 6 pieces of golden-brown toast |

Season the inside of the quails with salt and pepper, then stuff with the grapes (peeled). Truss, with a piece of pork fat around each quail.

Brown the quails quickly without other fat. Discard the melted fat and wipe the bottom of the pan.

Heat a heaped dessertspoon of butter in the pan and put back the quails, letting the butter sizzle. Sprinkle with marc, remove from the heat and cover, leaving the quails to absorb the alcohol.

Meanwhile, mash a third of the grapes, and thin the cornflour in the juice, pour over the quails, add salt, pepper and leave to simmer for 30 minutes on a low heat.

Peel the rest of the grapes and heat in a dessertspoon of butter until they are no longer transparent.

Fry the toast in the rest of the butter.

Remove the ties from the quails, arrange the toast on a serving dish and place a quail on each piece, surrounded by grapes, cover with sauce and serve immediately.

★★ PERNAND VERGELESSES 1991 - Clos Berthet Monopole
P. Dubreuil-Fontaine Père & Fils
*Fresh, light, and typical of Pernand, this excellent wine will add even more pleasure to this delicate dish.*

# CUISSOT DE SANGLIER RÔTI

## ROAST HAUNCH OF WILD BOAR

Preparation **20 min** 48 hrs before Cooking time **40 min** Equipment **roasting tin**

SERVES 6

1 haunch of about 2 kg
50 g melted butter
salt
MARINADE
2 dl red Burgundy
3 dessertspoons olive oil
1 dessertspoon Burgundy vinegar
freshly ground pepper
PEPPER SAUCE
1/2 l thick meat stock
100 g thinly sliced carrots
1/2 glass vinegar
1 thinly sliced medium onion
1 thinly sliced shallot
1 bay leaf
1 sprig of thyme
salt
freshly ground pepper
1/2 glass white Burgundy
1 glass stock

Place the haunch in a large terrine, add all the marinade ingredients and leave to steep for 48 hours. Drain the meat and pat dry, then smear all over with butter and place it in the roasting tin.

Put into a preheated hot oven (mark 8 / 230°C) for 40 minutes, season with salt and pepper and baste several times with the marinade during cooking.

Meanwhile, prepare the pepper sauce : Put the vinegar in a saucepan with the thyme, bay leaf, carrots, onion and shallot, reduce by half, then strain.

Make a thick meat stock, add the plain stock and some wine, add the vinegar reduction and leave to simmer for 35 minutes over a low heat.

Strain, add pepper, check seasoning.

When the boar is cooked, place it on a hot serving dish covered with its juices.

Serve accompanied by the pepper sauce.

★★ LADOIX 1ER CRU 1988 - Le clou d'Orge - Chevalier Père et Fils
*A wine whose animal character, as much in smell as in taste, makes it an ideal companion for red meat game.*

★★★★ BONNES MARES 1989 - Joseph Drouhin
*A very great wine whose power and structure are ideal for game like boar. An excellent wine for keeping.*

★★★★ POMMARD EPENOTS 1985 - H. de Montille
*A superb wine with a smell of autumnal undergrowth, perfect for boar.*

# LAPIN À LA BEAUNOISE

## BEAUNE-STYLE RABBIT

Preparation **30 min** the day before Cooking time **1 hr 30 min** Equipment **casse-**

SERVES 6

| | |
|---|---|
| 1 rabbit (approx 1.5 kg) | 1 small clove of garlic |
| MARINADE : | 2 cloves |
| 1 glass of oil | a pinch of cinnamon |
| 1 glass of red Côtes de Beaune wine | 1 bay leaf |
| 1 diced onion | salt |
| 1 diced shallot | freshly ground pepper |

Wash the rabbit and wipe it dry.

Cut into pieces, put them into a bowl then add all the ingredients for the marinade. Season with pepper, but not salt, mix well. Leave to marinate overnight.

The next day, put the pieces of rabbit into the casserole, pour over the marinade, add salt, cover and leave to cook over a low heat for 1 hour 30 minutes.

Remove and drain the pieces of rabbit, arrange on a serving dish, and keep hot.

Reduce the sauce and pour it over the rabbit.

*Serve with steamed potatoes.*

★ CHÂTEAU DE RULLY 1987 - Antonin Rodet

★★ CHÂTEAU DE RULLY 1990 - Antonin Rodet
*The aromas of ripe fruits suit the rabbit and spices in this recipe perfectly.*

★★★ CORTON BRESSANDES 1991 - Domaine J. Prieur
*A joyous, elegant wine with a slight liquorice quality which marries perfectly with the spices in the dish.*

# COQ AU JULIÉNAS

## COQ AU VIN

Preparation **40 min** the day before Cooking time **approx 2 hrs** Equipment **casserole**

### Serves 6

| | |
|---|---|
| 1 large chicken (about 4 kg) | 50 g redcurrant jelly |
| 2 bottles of wine (Juliénas) | 80 g flour |
| 2 tomatoes | 1 dl oil |
| 1 leek | 1 kg large button mushrooms |
| 3 onions | 200 g smoked bacon |
| 200 g carrots | 1 citron |
| 1 bouquet garni | salt |
| 2 cloves of garlic | freshly ground pepper |

Cut the chicken into pieces, then place in a large bowl.

Peel the vegetables, slice thinly, add to the bowl with the onions, garlic and the bouquet garni. Pour in the wine and leave to marinate for 24 hours.

The next day, drain the pieces of chicken, pat dry, then place in the casserole to fry in hot oil.

Remove the meat, discard the cooking oil, then put back the pieces of chicken, sprinkle with flour, stir and leave to brown. Add the marinade and the vegetables, redcurrant jelly, salt and pepper, mix well and leave to cook for about 2 hours.

Meanwhile, remove the ends of the mushroom stalks, wash quickly in water mixed with lemon juice, then cut into quarters and put aside.

Cut the bacon into dice and put aside.

Remove the chicken from the casserole and place on a serving dish. Keep in a warm place.

Strain the sauce, pour back into the casserole then add the mushrooms and bacon and leave to cook for a further 10 minutes.

Pour the sauce over the pieces of chicken and serve piping hot, with fresh pasta.

★★★ Faiveley 1991 - Nuits St Georges 1er cru - Les Forêts St Georges
*The complexity of this recipe will be sustained by the power of this excellent wine.*

# COQ SAUTÉ AUX VINS DE BOURGOGNE

## SAUTEED CHICKEN IN BURGUNDY SAUCE

Preparation **30 min** Cooking time **1 hr 30 to 2 hrs** Equipment **saucepan**

SERVES 4

1 free-range chicken (1.5 kg to 2 kg)
200 g unsmoked bacon
goose fat
2 carrots
2 onions
the green part of a leek (chopped)
1 l Burgundy :
1/3 white Burgundy
2/3 red Burgundy
6 peeled cloves of garlic
1 dessertspoon concentrated tomato purée
1 small bouquet garni
300 g mushrooms
2 dessertspoons butter
6 triangular croutons, fried in butter
1 dessertspoon finely chopped fines herbes

Cut off the neck of the chicken, remove the wings, breasts, legs and drumsticks,

Cut the neck and wings into two. Chop the carcass with any flesh attached into pieces.

COOKING THE SAUCE STOCK :

Fry the neck, ends of wings and carcass in the goose fat, then add the bacon and vegetables.

As soon as the mixture starts to cook, sprinkle with flour and brown. Add the wine and flambé.

Add the garlic, tomato, bouquet garni, leave to cook over a fairly low heat to reduce the sauce.

When cooked, there should only be just over a 1/2 litre of sauce left.

Strain the sauce, remove the fat carefully.

COOKING THE CHICKEN :

Fry the breasts, legs, drumsticks and wings on both sides then pour in the stock and cook slowly.

Meanwhile, clean the mushrooms, cut into quarters and cook in a pan with the butter, water, salt, some sugar, a little pepper and put aside.

Remove the pieces of chicken and keep warm. Strain the sauce, check seasoning, add a pinch of sugar and whisk in beurre manié (butter creamed with flour).

Put the pieces of chicken back into the finished sauce, with the bacon, mushrooms and small glazed onions, leave to reheat for a few moments.

Serve very hot garnished with croutons and sprinkled with fines herbes.

LE RÉCAMIER

★ DOMAINE DU CHÂTEAU DE MERCEY 1990 - (Santenay)
*This wine has much substance and honesty. It will highlight the flavours of the dish.*

★★★ CLOS DES SANTENOTS 1990 - (Volnay) - Domaine J. Prieur
*For the association of fine and tasty flavours with elegant aromas.*

★★★ VOLNAY SANTENOTS DU MILIEU 1989 - Domaine des Comtes Lafon
*A very rich wine, a little strong in alcohol content, which elegantly enhances the dish.*

★★★★ CLOS VOUGEOT 1991 - Domaine J. Prieur
*The quintessence of Burgundy aromas for this great regional speciality.*

# FRICASSÉE DE POULET À LA CRÈME

## CHICKEN FRICASSÉE WITH CREAM

Preparation **15 min** the day before **20 min** the next day
Cooking time **30 min** Equipment **deep frying pan**

SERVES 4

| | |
|---|---|
| 1 chicken (ready to cook, about 1.7 kg) | 1 sprig of thyme |
| a handful of cooking salt | 1 egg |
| 75 g butter | the juice of a lemon |
| 150 g small white onions | 20 cl fresh cream |
| 250 g wild mushrooms ; field mushrooms or meadow mushrooms | salt |
| | freshly ground pepper |

The day before, cut the chicken into 8 pieces (take out the small bones from the carcass), and sprinkle each piece with a little cooking salt, leave in a cool place.

The next day, wipe the pieces of chicken, peel the onions, then brown together in the deep frying pan with the butter.

Remove the chicken and onions, put aside, empty fat from pan. Clean the mushrooms and put into the frying pan with 25 g of butter, cover and leave to sweat for 3 to 4 minutes, then take them out with a skimmer, put aside.

Put the pieces of chicken into the frying pan with the onions and thyme, cover and cook for 15 minutes turning them once.

Remove the sprig of thyme, put back the mushrooms, add pepper, check seasoning and leave to simmer without a lid for 5 minutes. Mix the egg yolk with a good dash of lemon in a bowl, add 3 spoonfuls of cream and mix well.

Remove the pieces of chicken, onions and mushrooms with a skimmer, place on a serving dish and keep hot. Pour the cream mixture into the frying pan, mix briskly and pour over the pieces of meat.

*Associating cream, mushrooms and poultry is very common in Burgundy. In the past, verjuice was used for the sauce. Today, although verjuice has recently become available again, it is now replaced by lemon juice.*

☆☆ PULIGNY MONTRACHET 1992 - Clos de la Mouchère - 1er Cru - Volnay - J. Boillot
*A superb power which enhances white meats.*

☆☆ LADOIX 1991 - Côté de Beaune blanc - Chevalier
*A wine which is perfectly suited to mushrooms. It is very floral and slightly lemony in smell, at the same time being very fat in taste which goes well with poultry flesh.*

☆☆☆ CHÂTEAU DE RULLY 1986 - Antonin Rodet
*An excellent classic whose very vegetal taste suits poultry and mushrooms perfectly.*

# FAISAN AUX CHÂTAIGNES

## PHEASANT WITH CHESTNUTS

Preparation **30 min** Cooking time **1 hr 15 min** Equipment **casserole**

SERVES 4

| | |
|---|---|
| 1 pheasant (plucked and drawn) | 2 dl white Burgundy |
| 125 g foie gras | 1 liqueur glass brandy |
| 125 g lard | salt |
| 20 g flour | freshly ground pepper |
| 200 g chesnuts | 1 thin slice of pork fat |

Roughly mash the chesnuts, chop the foie gras, mix thoroughly, add salt and pepper. Stuff the pheasants with the foie gras mixture, truss and bard.

Cut the lard into cubes and melt in the casserole. Brown the pheasant on all sides then remove.

Sprinkle with flour and leave to fry for a few moments then add the wine, stir well and season with salt and pepper.

Put the pheasant back into the casserole, cover and leave to cook over a low heat for 1 hour 15 minutes. Check the cooking and turn over twice.

When cooked, carve the pheasant, arrange the pieces on a serving dish surrounded by slices of stuffing, keep in a warm place.

Strain the sauce, pour in the brandy, leave to reduce a little, check the seasoning and serve in a gravy boat.

★★★ BEAUNE CLOS DES MOUCHES ROUGE 1991 - Joseph Drouhin
*A wine with great finesse, essential for the chesnuts, a perfect balance.*

★★★ MOREY SAINT-DENIS 1990 - 1er Cru «Les Millandes» - Domaine Arlaud Père et Fils
*A magnificent wine, very concentrated and well-balanced, full of aromas of black fruits, which accompanies the autumnal flavours of the dish perfectly.*

# PINTADE AUX LENTILLES

## GUINEA FOWL WITH LENTILS

Preparation **20 min** Cooking time **30 min** Equipment **casserole and earthenware dish**

SERVES 2-3

1 guinea fowl (about 1 kg) ready to roast
40 g butter
1 dl chicken stock
2 dessertspoons poultry fat (or oil)
300 g Le Puy green lentils
1 large onion
1 bouquet garni
SAUCE
100 g lightly-salted bacon
2 dessertspoons of poultry fat
1 bouquet garni
1 thinly sliced large onion
1 dl chicken stock
1 dl veal stock with a little tomato
salt
freshly ground pepper
1 bunch of watercress for garnish

Coat the guinea fowl with the oil and fat, then place on its side in the dish. Place in a preheated moderate oven (mark 6 /180°C) and cook for 30 minutes. Turn several times during cooking.

Three-quarters through cooking, baste with hot chicken stock. Turn the bird onto its back to finish cooking and cover with aluminium foil.

Meanwhile, put the lentils into a saucepan of cold water, bring to the boil, add the bouquet garni and onion, cook slowly for 30 minutes. Add salt and pepper during cooking. As soon as the lentils are cooked, remove the bouquet garni and onion, drain and keep hot.

Prepare the sauce : cut the bacon into small cubes, boil for 5 minutes and cool.

Melt the poultry fat in a deep frying pan and fry the drained bacon until golden. Add the onion and fry until golden. Deglaze the pan immediately with the chicken stock.

Add the veal stock with tomato, mix carefully and leave to reduce by half, stirring from time to time with a spatula.

Place the guinea fowl, cut into halves on a hot serving dish, garnished with the bunch of watercress and pour over the remaining meat juices from the ovenproof dish.

Serve the lentils in a hot vegetable dish and the sauce in a gravy boat.

☆☆ CHÂTEAU DE CHAMIREY 1990 - Antonin Rodet
*Matches a very fine smell with a slightly mentholated freshness which suits the lentils perfectly.*

★★★ CORTON BRESSANDES 1991 - Domaine J. Prieur
*This wine is full of elegance and is a very good support for the lentils.*

# PINTADE À LA MATELOTTE

## GUINEA FOWL COOKED WITH HERBS AND RED WINE

Preparation **30 min** Cooking time **1 hr** Equipment **casserole**

SERVES 4

| | |
|---|---|
| 1 large, old guinea fowl (plucked and drawn) | 250 g button mushrooms |
| 2 medium-sized carrots | 1 bouquet garni |
| 2 medium-sized onions | 1 tin of anchovy fillets |
| 1 dessertspoon flour | 1 small tin of capers |
| 1 dl chicken stock | salt |
| 1 dl white Burgundy wine | freshly ground pepper |

Cut the guinea fowl into pieces and place in a casserole.

Peel and thinly slice the carrots and onions.

Fry the vegetables with the butter until golden then sprinkle with flour, stir briskly and add the stock and wine. Mix well and boil for 10 minutes.

Strain this roux and add part to the pieces of guinea fowl with the bouquet garni, salt, and pepper. Cover and simmer for 30 minutes.

Remove the ends of the mushroom stalks, wash quickly in cold water and dry, then cut into two or three depending on size.

Turn over the pieces of guinea fowl, add the mushrooms and leave to simmer for another 20 minutes.

Cut the anchovy fillets into thin strips.

When the dish is cooked, remove the bouquet garni, add the capers and anchovies, mix carefully. Bring to a simmer, stirring constantly and cook for 5 minutes.

Serve on a hot dish with steamed potatoes.

☆☆☆ PULIGNY-MONTRACHET 1992 - Les Combettes - Etienne Sauzet
*Very typical of the Pulignys, its depth and power are in perfect harmony with the dish.*

# PERDREAUX AUX MORILLES

## PARTRIDGE WITH MOREL MUSHROOMS

Preparation **40 min** Cooking time **30 min** Equipment **roasting tin**

SERVES 6

| | |
|---|---|
| 3 young partidges (plucked) | 1 bunch of parsley |
| 3 thin slices of pork fat | 1 sprig of thyme |
| 100 g morel mushrooms | 2 liqueur glasses of Burgundy marc |
| 100 g lard | salt, freshly ground pepper |
| 100 g butter | 6 slices of farmhouse bread |
| 4 chicken livers | (with the crusts removed) |

Clean out the partridges (put the livers aside) and season inside with salt and pepper. Wash the morels under cold water, dry carefully, put aside.

Next, put all the livers in a frying pan with a knob of butter, seize them and let them harden for a few minutes over a medium heat, then drain and chop with the lard, thyme (rubbed) and the sliced morels.

Sprinkle the mixture with marc, add salt and pepper and check seasoning. Put aside. Place a knob of butter and a heaped dessertspoon of stuffing inside each bird, then sew up, truss and bard and place the partridges in the roasting tin.

Roast in a preheated hot oven (mark 7 / 200°C) for 30 minutes. Turn the birds twice so that they cook evenly, and baste with a little water. When cooked, flambé with marc, switch off the oven and leave to absorb their juices for 5 minutes.

Meanwhile, fry the slices of bread (with the crusts removed) with some butter, until golden brown, then spread with stuffing and place on the serving dish. Keep hot.

Remove the bards from the partridges, cut into halves and place each half on a slice of fried bread.

Serve accompanied by the meat juices in a gravy boat.

★★★ BEAUNE CLOS DES MOUCHES ROUGE 1991 - Joseph Drouhin
*A delicate and feminine wine which suits the finesse of the game perfectly.*

☆☆☆☆ CORTON-CHARLEMAGNE 1992 - Grand Cru - Chevalier Père et Fils
*For those who like a white wine with morel mushrooms, this wine, typical of Corton, will be perfect, thanks to its mineral content and powerful taste. Excellent wine for keeping.*

# PERDRIX AUX CHOUX

## PARTRIDGE WITH CABBAGE

Preparation **30 min** Cooking time **2 hrs** Equipment **casserole**

SERVES 4

2 partridges (plucked and drawn)
3 thin slices of pork fat
300 g bacon cut into cubes
1 Morteau sausage
200 g shoulder of veal cut into pieces
3 small cabbages
3 onions stuck with cloves
3 carrots
1 bay leaf
salt
freshly ground pepper

Blanch the cabbages, drain well, then tie up.

Bard the partridges with the pork fat, place them into the casserole and sprinkle with bacon. Add the pieces of veal and the sausage.

Add the onions, carrots and a bay leaf to the partridges, then lay the cabbages on top, cover with the last slice of pork fat. Cover and leave to simmer on a low heat for 2 hours.

Then, take out the partridges and remove the slices of pork fat. Cut the birds in half, place on a serving dish and keep hot.

Drain the cabbages, untie and arrange them around the partridges, garnished with slices of Morteau sausage and pieces of veal. Sprinkle with bacon.

Then strain the cooking juices, add pepper, check seasoning which should be quite spicy and servc in a gravy boat.

☆☆☆☆ CORTON-CHARLEMAGNE 1992 - Grand Cru - Chevalier Père et Fils
*The mineral nature of this excellent wine suits both the partridge flesh and the texture of the cabbage.*

★★★★ VOSNE ROMANÉE 1990 - 1er Cru les Petits Monts - Mongeard -Mugneret
*This wine, very representative of its appelation matches power and finesse and goes well with this recipe. Excellent wine for keeping.*

# PETITS POULETS À LA BEAUNOISE

## BEAUNE - STYLE CHICKEN

Preparation **25 min** Cooking time **30 min** Equipment **deep pan**

SERVES 8

| | |
|---|---|
| 2 corn-fed chickens (approx 1.2 kg each) | salt |
| 125 g butter | freshly ground pepper |
| 20 small onions (the same size) | PILLAU RICE |
| 2 crushed cloves of garlic | 400 g rice |
| 1 bouquet garni | 2 dessertspoons oil |
| 1 dl Nouilly Prat | 2 dessertspoons butter |
| 1/2 bottle Aligoté Burgundy | 1 large chopped onion |
| 1 teaspoon arrowroot | 1 l chicken stock |
| 1 dessertspoon white wine | 1 bouquet garni |
| 50 cl fresh cream | salt and pepper |

Dissolve the arrowroot in the white wine, put aside. Peel the small onions, put aside.

Divide the chickens into four, season with salt and pepper, then butter the pan generously and add the pieces of chicken, small onions and bouquet garni.

Cover and leave to sweat over a low heat for 5 minutes.

Turn the meat over, add the garlic, cover and leave to sweat for another 5 minutes until the chicken is golden brown. Remove the onions, glaze and put aside.

Sprinkle the Nouilly Prat and white wine over the chicken, cover, place on a high heat for a few moments then reduce the heat and cook for 25 minutes.

Next, add the cream and leave to simmer for another 5 minutes. Arrange the pieces of chicken on a serving dish, surrounded by the glazed onions, keep hot.

Remove the bouquet garni and the garlic (if it hasn't melted), reduce the sauce then add the dissolved arrowroot, bring to the boil quickly while whisking, and immediately pour over the pieces of chicken.

Serve with Pillau rice prepared separately.

LE RÉCAMIER

☆☆ PULIGNY-MONTRACHET 1992 - Clos de la Mouchère 1er cru - J. Boillot
*A superb power which enhances white meats.*

☆☆☆ MEURSAULT-CHARMES 1989 - Domaine des Comtes Lafon
*A superb wine which highlights the finesse of the young chickens.*

# POULET AUX GIROLLES

## CHICKEN WITH CHANTERELLES

Preparation **25 min** Cooking time **50 min** Equipment **deep pan**

SERVES 5-6

2 farm-bred chickens
1 kg fresh chanterelle mushrooms
4 chopped shallots
1 clove of garlic
1 bunch of chopped parsley
1 teaspoon of rubbed thyme
4 dessertspoons oil
25 g butter
salt
freshly ground pepper

Remove the earthy ends of the chanterelle stalks, wash several times in cold water with a little vinegar added. Dry very carefully in a tea-towel, put aside.

Cut the chickens into pieces.

Heat 2 dessertspoons of oil in the deep pan and fry the pieces of meat, then remove them as they are browned.

Once all the pieces of chicken are browned, fry half of the chopped shallots until soft, stir well and put the meat back into the pan, sprinkled with thyme, salt and pepper. Cover and cook over a low heat for 35 minutes.

Meanwhile, fry the chanterelles with the rest of the oil until the juice has evaporated.

Then add the butter and the chopped parsley, garlic, remaining shallots, salt and pepper. Cook for 10 minutes on a moderate heat then add the chicken covered with chanterelles and leave to cook for a further 10 minutes.

Serve on a hot dish.

☆ SANTENAY 1991 - Clos de Malte - Louis Jadot
*This wine is fat and mineral at the same time. Its pronounced bouquet of undergrowth suits the chanterelle and the flavour of the poultry.*

★★★ CHAMBOLLE-MUSIGNY 1990 - Domaine Arlaud Père et Fils
*The elegance of this wine suits the chanterelles. Its finesse harmonizes well with the poultry.*

# POULARDE DE BRESSE DEMI-DEUIL

Preparation **40 min** Cooking time **1 hr 15 min** Equipment **large saucepan**

SERVES 4

1 white poularde (fattened chicken) weighing 2 kg (drawn & cleaned)
4 l chicken stock
100 g trimmed baby carrots
100 g celery
1 bunch young leeks
60 g flour
60 g butter (for a beurre manié)
2 dl fresh cream
STUFFING
100 g fresh truffles
65 g pork
65 g veal
65 g mushrooms
the liver of the poularde
2 spoonfuls cognac
1 bouquet garni
white peppercorns
1 pig's bladder
1 dl good white wine
salt

Remove the head and neck of the poularde, and the two feet with the leg bone without tearing the flesh.

Mince together the pork, veal, mushrooms and chicken liver. Add some of the truffles having chopped them first, and sprinkle with cognac. Mix carefully and stuff the bird, sewing it up afterwards.

Then, slice the remaining truffle thinly. Insert the slices carefully between the flesh and skin of the poularde and truss.

Place the bird inside the pig's bladder, which has been thoroughly washed in tepid water. Season with salt, pepper and spices, sprinkle with white wine.

Tie up the bladder carefully, and cook in a court-bouillon prepared earlier with vegetables. Leave to cook for 1 hour 15 minutes.

Remove the pigs bladder and serve the poularde surrounded by vegetables on a hot serving dish.

☆☆☆ MONTRACHET 1990 - Domaine J. Prieur
*Full, powerful and elegant. A wine with a great personality for a refined dish.*

☆☆☆ PULIGNY-MONTRACHET 1992 - «Les Combettes» Etienne Sauzet
*The truffle in this dish will be perfectly enhanced by this rich, deep, powerful wine which is full of breeding.*

★★★★ FAIVELEY 1989 - Mazis-Chambertin
*The Mazis is the greatest of the Chambertin crus. It is a perfect, elegant wine, which has a very lovely smell and subtle aromas. Perfect for this great dish.*

# RÂBLE DE LIÈVRE À LA CRÈME

## SADDLE OF HARE WITH CREAM

Preparation **10 min** the day before **20 min** the next day Cooking time **45 min** Equipment **roasting tin**

SERVES 4

| | |
|---|---|
| Saddle of a large hare | MARINADE |
| 1 thin slice of pork fat | 1 bottle white Macon wine |
| 60 g butter | 1 dessertspoon vinegar |
| 1 liqueur glass of Burgundy marc | 1 bouquet garni |
| 100 g fresh cream | 6 crushed peppercorns |
| salt, freshly ground pepper | |

The day before, put the hare into a terrine, sprinkle with wine, add the vinegar, bouquet garni and pepper. Leave to marinate overnight in a cool place.

The next day dry the meat carefully and cover with the pork fat, season with salt and pepper. Place the hare in the roasting tin and cook in a preheated hot oven (mark 7 / 200°C) for 45 minutes.

Check cooking and baste with melted butter and the marinade.

Then remove the joint and place on a hot serving dish.

Deglaze the tin and flambé with the marc. Mix the juice with the cream, stir well without letting the liquid boil. Check seasoning.

Serve the hare accompanied with the sauce in a gravy boat and a cranberry sauce prepared separately.

★★★ CHAMBOLLE-MUSIGNY 1990 - Domaine Arlaud Père et Fils

*This very typical wine from Chambolle is very pleasant and fruity. Its finesse will bring out the strengths of the hare.*

# RÔTI DE MARCASSIN

## ROAST YOUNG WILD BOAR WITH BURGUNDY SAUCE

Preparation **20 min** Cooking time **35 min** Equipment **casserole**

SERVES 6

750 g saddle of young wild boar
150 g cubes of bacon
30 g butter
1/4 l good white Burgundy
15 cl fresh cream
salt, freshly ground pepper
MARINADE
1 bottle of good red Burgundy
1 liqueur glass of Burgundy marc
2 carrots cut into quarters
1 stick of celery
2 bay leaves
2 cloves of garlic
the juice of a lemon
1 teaspoon freshly ground pepper

Put all the ingredients for the marinade in an earthenware bowl, then add the saddle of boar and leave to marinate for 24 hours.

The next day, take out the meat, dry it carefully and place in the casserole with the butter and bacon. Brown the meat, add salt, pepper, cover and cook for 35 minutes, turning the saddle several times.

Remove the meat and bacon, keep hot.

Remove the cooking fat and pour in the marc and white wine. Reduce then add the cream and stir carefully, thicken, check seasoning.

Serve the saddle of boar on a hot dish, surrounded by the bacon and the sauce in a gravy boat.

*This dish is delicious served with a gratin of potatoes. The remaining marinade can be used for another dish.*

★ DOMAINE DES HAUTES CORNIÈRES
Chassagne-Montrachet 1er cru 1990 - Morgeot - P. Chapelle et Fils
*A good wine for keeping. Powerful, it has slightly cooked aromas which will suit the strong flavour of the young boar perfectly.*

# FISH

*Among fish dishes, how can we overlook
" Pouchouse " or Pauchouse, kind of matelote
in white wine, which was the glory of Verdun on
the Doubs, Meurette, matelote in red wine from
the banks of the Saône.*

*Discover dijon pike fillets,
and the typically Burgundian pike quenelles,
pike mousse with Nantua sauce,
not forgetting Burgundy eel.*

# ANGUILLE BOURGUIGNONNE

## BURGUNDY-STYLE EEL

Preparation **15 min** Cooking time **20 min** Equipment **frying pan**

SERVES 6

1 eel (medium-size)
a court-bouillon with wine wine
2 eggs
25 g butter
salt
freshly ground pepper
mustard mayonnaise

Cut the eel into thick slices, cook in the court-bouillon and then leave to cool completely.

Roll the slices in beaten egg and fry in butter.

Serve hot with a mayonnaise made with plenty of mustard.

☆☆☆ CHÂTEAU FUISSÉ 1993 - Les Brûlés - J.J. Vincent
*Superb wine, with a full flavour, having at the same time strength and finesse. Everything needed for this traditional dish.*

# BRÈME AU GRATIN

## BREAM AU GRATIN

Preparation **1 hr** Cooking time **25 min** Equipment **ovenproof earthenware dish**

SERVES 4

1 large bream
3 dessertspoons of oil
100 g salted bacon
1 bunch of chopped fresh sorrel
1 crushed clove of garlic
1 chopped onion
2 chopped shallots
1 bunch of chopped parsley
1 knob of butter
15 cl fresh cream
salt
freshly ground pepper
1 heaped dessertspoon of breadcrumbs

Clean out the bream, wash thoroughly under cold water and dry carefully.

Snip the most rounded part of the back, then marinate in oil for 30 minutes.

Chop the bacon into small cubes, then mix thoroughly with the garlic, onion, shallots and sorrel. Add the butter, cream, pepper. Check seasoning (remember that the bacon is already salted).

Stuff the fish with this mixture and sew up.

Place the bream on the ovenproof dish with the remaining stuffing on its back.

Sprinkle with breadcrumbs, then cook in a preheated hot oven (mark 7 / 200°C) for about 25 minutes until crispy and golden.

★★★★ VOSNE ROMANÉE 1990 - 1er Cru les Petits Monts - Mongeard Mugneret
*This powerful wine will enhance the fish, while its finesse avoids overshadowing it.*

# COQUILLES SAINT-JACQUES

## SCALLOPS WITH CARAMELISED CHICORY

Preparation **25 min** Infusion **30 min** Cooking time **25 min** Equipment **3 deep frying pans**

Serves 4

| | |
|---|---|
| 16 to 20 scallops (according to size) | 1 dessertspoon oil |
| 6 heads of chicory | 1 dl fish stock (prepared in advance, or instant) |
| 2 dessertspoons of sherry | 2 sprigs of tarragon |
| 280 g butter (fresh, from a block) | salt |
| 1 dessertspoon honey | small black peppercorns (crushed) |

Make clarified butter : heat 100 g of butter until it melts, skim and put aside.

Cut the chicory into julienne strips, soften over a high heat in a frying pan with a knob of butter, season with salt and peppercorns, put aside.

Meanwhile, in another frying pan, cook the scallops in the clarified butter over a low heat, with a drop of oil, keep hot.

Caramelize the honey in another frying pan, mix with sherry vinegar then add the fish stock and whisk the sauce with knobs of butter until it becomes smooth. Add the tarragon and leave for 30 minutes so that the flavour is absorbed, (in a bain-marie or double saucepan).

Check seasoning.

Serve on individual plates; first some sauce, then the chicory in the middle surrounded by scallops.

☆ Domaine de Bongran - Cuvée tradition - J. Thévenet
*A very elegant wine which has a fat side, slightly coralline at initial contact and with an acid finish, which suits this dish.*

☆☆☆ Mâcon Clessé 1987
Domaine de Bongran - Cuvée Spéciale Levrouté - J. Thévenet
*Well-rounded and soft, this wine is in perfect harmony with the caramelized chicory.*

# BROCHET AU BEURRE BLANC

## PIKE WITH BEURRE BLANC

Preparation **20 min** Cooking time **25 min** Equipment **fish kettle**

SERVES 6

1 large pike (cleaned, scales removed)
COURT-BOUILLON
2 to 3 l water (according to the size of the pike)
2 dl Pouilly wine
50 g thinly sliced carrots
1 large onion cut in half
1 clove
1 sprig of parsley
salt, freshly ground pepper

BEURRE BLANC
Preparation : 5 minutes
Cooking time : 15 minutes
1 glass of Pouilly wine
2 shallots
250 g butter
salt
peppercorns

Place the pike in the fish kettle and cover with court-bouillon. Bring to the boil and simmer for 25 minutes.

Remove the fish and skin, keeping it warm.

Peel the shallots and blend to a purée. Place the shallots in a small saucepan with the wine over a low heat, until the wine has almost completely evaporated.

Lower the heat as much as possible, and whisk in the butter little by little. At first, the sauce should look like a custard, then thicken slightly. Season with salt and pepper. Be very careful not to let the sauce boil. Keep it warm in a bain-marie (or a double saucepan).

Serve the pike on a serving dish garnished with a folded napkin or clean cloth, with the sauce in a gravy boat.

☆☆ LADOIX 1991 - Côte de Beaune Blanc
*This very floral and opulent wine enhances the pike flesh.*

☆☆ BEAUNE CLOS DES MOUCHES 1992 - Chanson Père et Fils
*This clear, balanced wine is still very discreet and its finesse adapts well to the pike flesh.*

☆☆☆ MEURSAULT PERRIÈRES 1991 - Joseph Drouhin
*A spiritual wine, very typical of the hillside wines whose sunny flavours will bring out the very best of the pike.*

# MOUSSE DE BROCHET SAUCE NANTUA

## PIKE MOUSSE WITH NANTUA SAUCE

Preparation **1 hr 35 min** Cooking time **40 & 40 min** Equipment **terrine mould and casserole**

SERVES 8

1 large pike
500 g butter
1/2 l fresh cream
4 whole eggs
4 egg yolks
salt
freshly ground pepper
cayenne pepper

NANTUA SAUCE
2 l fish stock
2 kg live crayfish
2 carrots
2 leeks
300 g shallots
1 bouquet garni with tarragon
1 dessertspoon olive oil
1 glass of brandy
2 dessertspoons of concentrated tomato purée
1/2 l white wine
120 g butter
120 g flour
2 spoonfuls of fresh cream
salt
cayenne pepper

PIKE MOUSSE :

Remove the bones from the pike, obtaining 500 g of flesh.

Blend the fish on a slow speed in a food processor, and season with salt and pepper while blending.

Once the flesh is smooth, add the butter in small knobs, mix well, then add the whole eggs and the 4 yolks while beating constantly, ensuring that the mixture remains smooth.

Place in a large bowl and using a spoon, carefully fold in the cream.

Butter the mould and fill with mousse to 1 cm from the top.

Cook in a bain-marie (place the mould in a baking tin half-filled with water) in a pre-heated hot oven (mark 7 / 200°C) for 40 minutes.

Leave to rest for 10 minutes.

You can use individual soufflé moulds, in which case the cooking time in a bain-marie will be 20 minutes at the same temperature.

NANTUA SAUCE

The mirepoix : peel, wash and chop the carrots, leeks and shallots, put aside.

Separate the head and tails of the crayfish, put aside.

# MOUSSE DE BROCHET SAUCE NANTUA

Make the fish stock in a saucepan with 2 1/2 litres water and 1 sachet of fish stock. Bring to the boil then add the crayfish tails. Cook for 3 to 4 minutes. Remove, cool and peel.

Prepare the beurre manié, creaming 120 g of butter by hand with 120 g of flour until a smooth paste is obtained, put aside.

Heat the olive oil in a large casserole then add the crayfish heads and cook at a high heat for 10 minutes, mashing well.

Pour in the brandy, flambé, then add the mirepoix, tomato concentrate, crushed garlic cloves, mix carefully and leave to cook for 15 minutes.

Next add the fish stock and white wine, add the bouquet garni, salt and pepper and leave to cook for 40 minutes.

Blend the mixture to obtain a smooth purée, or use a vegetable mill.

Pour the stock into a saucepan, bring to the boil, then mix in the beurre manié in small knobs until the desired consistency is obtained.

Strain and check seasoning. Finally add the cream and crayfish tails. Keep hot in a bain marie.

LE RÉCAMIER

☆☆☆ CHÂTEAU DE RULLY 1989 - Antonin Rodet
*Round, fat, slightly honeyed and perfectly suited to the richness of this recipe.*

☆☆☆ BEAUNE CLOS DES MOUCHES 1992 - Joseph Drouhin
*This wine has a pleasant smell full of freshness and elegance. Its power in the mouth suits the strength of the crayfish sauce perfectly.*

# FILETS DE BROCHET DIJONNAISE

## DIJON PIKE FILLETS

Preparation **25 min** the day before Cooking time **20 min** Equipment **earthenware dish**

SERVES 6

| | |
|---|---|
| 1 pike (approx 2 kg) | 6 shallots |
| 125 g lard | 1 bunch of parsley |
| 250 g butter | 1 bouquet garni |
| 250 g button mushrooms | 10 cl fresh cream |
| 1/2 bottle white wine | salt |
| 3 cl Burgundy marc | freshly ground pepper |

Fillet the pike when raw, wash, pat dry, dot with lard and place in a dish.

Pour the white wine and marc over the fish, add the peeled and halved shallots, bouquet garni, salt and pepper. Cover and leave to marinate for 24 hours.

The next day, remove the ends of the mushroom stalks, wash quickly, dry and chop with the parsley. Mix well and put aside.

Butter the dish generously then spread the mushroom mixture over the bottom of the dish and place the pike fillets on top.

Next, strain the marinade and pour over the fish.

Cook in a preheated hot oven (mark 7 / 200°C) for 20 minutes until golden brown.

Just before serving, cover with cream and a few knobs of butter.

☆☆☆ PULIGNY-MONTRACHET 1992 - Les Combettes - Etienne Sauzet
*This very expressive, well-structured wine accompanies this dish with elegance.*

# QUENELLES DE BROCHET

## PIKE QUENELLES

Preparation **25 min** Cooking time **15 min** Equipment **earthenware bowl and small pan**

SERVES 4

| | |
|---|---|
| 70 g butter | 4 eggs |
| 100 g flour | 300 g flaked pike |
| 30 cl milk | salt and pepper |

Flake the pike or blend roughly, put aside. Boil the milk and add the butter.

Put the flour into the bowl, then pour in the milk whisking constantly.

Put the mixture onto the heat and leave to cook until almost dry, stirring all the while. Next, add 2 eggs one by one, whisking hard, then leave to cool. Add the pike flesh and the 2 other eggs, beating the mixture hard, then strain.

Using a spoon, form the quenelles and poach for 15 minutes in boiling salty water (or fish stock). Take them out as they rise to the surface, drain and keep hot.

Serve with nantua sauce (or chablis sauce).

Prepare nantua sauce :

1/3 l bechamel sauce

2 dl cream

60 g crayfish butter (or if not, a tin of crayfish bisque)

salt and freshly ground pepper

Make a bechamel sauce, add 1 decilitre of cream and warm over a low heat. Mix well, add salt and pepper.

Add another decilitre of fresh cream, then 60 g seafood butter. Check seasoning and cover the quenelles with the sauce.

☆ FAIVELEY 1993 - Hautes Côtes de Nuits «Dames Huguettes»
*A wine with a both delicate and powerful smell whose taste can match that of the pike.*

# BRANDADE DE MORUE

## COD BRANDADE

Preparation **35 min** Cooking time **10 min & 15 min** Equipment **large saucepan and small pan**

SERVES 6

1 kg salted and dried cod
600 g potatoes (for mashing)
1/2 l olive oil
40 cl cream
4 cloves of garlic
salt
pepper
2 cl truffle juice and thin slices of truffles (to taste)

Soak the cod overnight, in slowly running water. Drain the cod, then cut into pieces of the same size. Place in the large saucepan with 4 to 5 litres of water. Bring to the boil and continue to simmer for 10 minutes.

Take out the pieces of fish and remove the skin and bones.

Flake the cod (leave a little jelly-like white skin so that the brandade is smooth) and put aside.

Meanwhile, cook the potatoes in their skins, as for mashing. Drain and peel, push through a sieve and put aside.

Heat the oil with the crushed garlic cloves, leave to absorb the flavour and sieve.

Bring the cream to the boil, put aside.

Mix the potatoes with the flaked cod and garlic. Stir well to remove any remaining lumps until the mixture is smooth. Add a little pepper.

Then add the hot cream. Mix well so that the mixture is creamy and even smoother. Just before serving, add the truffle juice and sprinkle with the truffle slices.

Taste, check seasoning and serve.

LE RÉCAMIER

☆ FAIVELEY 1993 - Hautes Côtes de Nuit «Dames Huguettes»
*A wine with a delicate smell, but structured enough to balance the texture of the brandade.*

☆☆ LADOIX 1993 - Les Gréchons - Chevalier Père et Fils
*An attractive honeyed smell, flattering, which softens the rustic aspect of the brandade.*

# LA MEURETTE DE BOURGOGNE

## FISH IN A BURGUNDY SAUCE

Preparation **30 min** Cooking time **35 min** Equipment **thick-based saucepan**

SERVES 4

small eel, small pike, carp, trout
(freshly caught)
1 l red Burgundy wine
1 large onion stuck with a clove
1 bouquet garni
4 crushed garlic cloves
1 bunch of parsley
approx 50 g beurre manié
(butter creamed with flour to a smooth paste)
25 g butter
2 liqueur glasses of brandy
salt
freshly ground pepper
4 slices of farmhouse bread

Clean the fish and cut into thick slices. Pour the wine into the saucepan, bring to the boil, add the onion, bouquet garni, garlic and slices of fish which should be just covered by the liquid.

Bring back to the boil on a high heat, add the brandy and flambé. Cook for 20 minutes, then remove the saucepan from the heat and mix the beurre manié into the sauce. Replace on a low heat and simmer for a further 10 minutes.

Remove the pan from the heat, strain the sauce and add the butter in knobs. Keep warm.

Grill the slices of bread, rub with garlic, sprinkle with melted butter and arrange in a serving dish.

Place the fish onto the toast, cover with sauce and serve.

*Meurette is a very traditional dish in Burgundy*

★ SAVIGNY-LES-BEAUNE 1er CRU 1992 - Les Marconnets - Simon Bize et Fils
*Very lively, with a slightly leafy quality, this Savigny will pleasantly refresh and give spirit to this dish.*

★★ PERNAND-VERGELESSES 1991
Clos Berthet Monopole - Domaine P. Dubreuil-Fontaine Père et Fils
*Excellent wine, very typical of the area. Very fine and pleasant to drink, suits this traditional meurette perfectly.*

★★★ GEVREY-CHAMBERTIN 1992 - Domaine Armand Rousseau Père et Fils
*A great and powerful wine which will glorify the meurette.*

# FILETS DE SOLES AU VIN ROUGE

## SOLE FILLETS IN RED WINE

Preparation **30 min** Cooking time **10 min** Equipment **ovenproof dish**

SERVES 6

3 soles (800 g each)
SAUCE
5 to 6 shallots
1 stick of celery
2 leeks (white part only)
250 g button mushrooms
1 bouquet garni
100 g butter
40 g flour
1 bottle red wine
salt
freshly ground pepper

Fillet the soles, the roll them up and place in the buttered dish.

Peel,wash and slice the mushrooms thinly, and place in a saucepan with 1/4 litre of water. Season with salt and pepper and cook slowly for 20 minutes.

Next, prepare the fish stock :

Sweat the fish bones in another saucepan with butter for 10 minutes, with the shallots, leeks, celery and bouquet garni. Add the wine and mushroom juices (kept to one side), leave to cook slowly for 20 minutes.

Strain the liquid onto the sole fillets and poach for 10 minutes. Remove and keep them in a warm place.

Reduce the sauce by half, mix in a little beurre manié (butter creamed with flour to a smooth paste), the mushrooms and the rest of the butter.

Check seasoning.

Cover the fillets with the hot sauce.

★ CHÂTEAU DE MERCEY 1990 - Mercurey - 1er Cru en Sazenay
*The fine tannin of this wine suits the delicate flavour of the sole admirably.*

★★ CHÂTEAU DE RULLY 1990 - Antonin Rodet
*A delicate bouquet, perfect for the fish.*

★★ SAINT-ROMAIN 1990 - Alain Gras
*A red wine of great finesse, perfectly suited to the delicate flesh of the sole.*

# RAIE À LA MOUTARDE

## SKATE IN A MUSTARD SAUCE

Preparation **35 min** Cooking time **8 min** Equipment **couscous pan or steamer**

SERVES 8

| | |
|---|---|
| 1.2 kg skate | 100 g seaweed |
| 200 g butter | 2 dl fresh cream |
| 2 onions | 2 dessertspoons strong mustard |
| 1 stick of celery | 1 pot of capers |
| 1 leek (white part) | salt |
| 1 bouquet garni | freshly ground pepper |

In a deep pan, make a fish stock with the onions cut into quarters, the leek, celery, bouquet garni and seaweed.

Add the two litres of water and white wine and cook for 20 minutes over a low heat. Then steam the skate using this stock for 8 minutes.

Mix the butter, cream and 2 dl of fish stock to obtain a smooth mixture. Bring to the boil, then add the butter little by little and stir in the mustard thoroughly.

Arrange the skate on a hot serving dish, sprinkle with capers, cover with the sauce and add a pinch of chervil and parsley.

Serve immediately.

LE RÉCAMIER

☆☆ PULIGNY-MONTRACHET 1992 - Clos de la Mouchère - 1er Cru - J. Boillot
*A powerful Volnay whose acidity suits the mustard sauce well.*

☆☆ CHÂTEAU DE RULLY 1992 - Antonin Rodet
*An excellent classic, as suitable for inclusion in this dish as to accompany it.*

# PAUCHOUSE

Preparation **35 min** | Cooking time **35 min** | Equipment **casserole**

SERVES 6

| | |
|---|---|
| 250 g eel | 2 egg yolks |
| 250 g carp | 1 onion |
| 250 g pike | 2 cloves of garlic |
| 1 bottle white Aligoté wine | 1 bouquet garni |
| 1 dl Burgundy marc | salt |
| 150 g butter | freshly ground pepper |
| 15 cl fresh cream | |

Remove the scales, clean out and wash the fish. Cut into thick slices. Boil the wine in the casserole and add the slices of fish with the garlic, onion and bouquet garni, 50 g of butter, salt and pepper.

After 10 minutes, add the marc and flambé, then simmer for 35 minutes over a low heat.

Mix the sauce, remaining butter, cream and egg yolks. Stir quickly.

Serve on a hot dish, accompanied with small croutons fried in butter.

★ PINOT DE VIEILLES VIGNES 1990 - Bourgogne- Antonin Rodet
*A classic which pleasantly highlights this traditional dish.*

★★ SAINT-ROMAIN 1990 - Alain Gras
*A delicate wine which enhances the flesh of the different fish.*

# DESSERTS

*Specialities of Burgundy patisserie are famous : nonnettes and spicy bread with glacé fruit.*

*The Burgundy area produces many cakes and gateaux, the best-known being fruit tarts, more often called 'flans', with blackcurrant, rhubarb etc...*

*Among local gateaux, simple pancakes also called Matefaim, Burgundy crunchies, Cluny tartouillat with fruit...*

*Taste the refined dijon pears, or the sublime Récamier apple tart and enjoy yourselves !*

# CLAFOUTIS DE VINZELLES

## VINZELLES CLAFOUTIS

Preparation **20 min** Cooking time **35 min** Equipment **ovenproof clafoutis mould**

SERVES 6

700 g strawberries
220 g flour
4 eggs
160 g caster sugar
50 g butter
a pinch of salt
1/2 l warmed milk

Hull the strawberries, put aside.

Melt the butter in a double saucepan. Put the flour into a bowl, add sugar (keep 2 dessertspoons to sprinkle over the clafoutis), the pinch of salt and mix well.

Make a well in the centre and break the eggs into it one by one, beat well and add the melted butter, beating constantly.

Add the warm milk gradually, mix thoroughly to obtain a smooth batter.

Grease the mould well, arrange the strawberries on the base of the mould and pour over the batter.

Cook in a preheated moderate oven (mark 6 / 180°C) for 35 minutes. When cooked, the clafoutis should come away from the sides of the mould.

Sprinkle with the rest of the caster sugar and serve quite hot.

# CROQUETS BOURGUIGNONS

## BURGUNDY CRUNCHIES

Preparation **15 min** Cooking time **15 min** Equipment **rectangular tart mould**

SERVES 4

| | |
|---|---|
| 3 eggs<br>225 g flour<br>225 g sugar<br>a pinch of salt | 1/2 sachet baking powder<br>100 g shelled hazelnuts<br>butter to grease the mould |

Grill the nuts lightly, then chop roughly.

Beat the eggs in a bowl with the sugar and a pinch of salt. While stirring, sprinkle in the flour and baking powder.

Next add the hazelnuts and mix well.

Grease the mould carefully and fill with the mixture. Cook in a moderate oven (mark 6 /180°C) for 15 minutes.

When cooked, remove the mould from the oven and while still hot, cut into diamond shapes.

Leave the crunchies to harden in the mould.

*These crunchies are particularly delicious at tea-time.*

# FLAN AU CASSIS

## BLACKCURRANT FLAN

Preparation **25 min** Cooking time **45 min** Equipment **earthenware casserole & tart mould**

SERVES 6

1 kg blackcurrants
250 g shortcrust pastry
300 g caster sugar
1 dessertspoon of semolina
2 dessertspoons of fresh cream

Prepare the shortcrust pastry, put aside.

Put the blackcurrants into the casserole with a large glass of water. Heat until the blackcurrants split open.

Blend the fruit, then boil for 5 minutes.

Squeeze to extract the blackcurrant juice, add the sugar and boil for 15 minutes.

Line the mould with the pastry, spread the semolina over the surface and pour over the blackcurrant jelly.

Place in a preheated hot oven (fan oven mark 7 / 200°C) for 40 to 45 minutes.

When cooked, leave until completely cold, then spread with cream before serving.

# LA TARTE AUX POMMES

## APPLE TART

Preparation **10 min** the day before **2 hrs** the next day Cooking time **30 min**
Equipment **pâtisserie board and baking tray**

SERVES 6

| | |
|---|---|
| 500 g flour | 180 g butter (to spread over the dough) |
| 250 g butter | 1 kg Golden Delicious apples |
| 1 dl 85 water | 150 g caster sugar |
| a pinch of salt | 100 g apricot jam |

Place the flour and the pinch of salt in a ring shape on the board, then pour a mixture of the melted butter and cold water into the well in the centre.

Knead hard to obtain a smooth dough. Form a ball and place it in the refrigerator for 12 hours. This mixture is called " détrempe ".

The next day, place the dough onto the floured board, roll out into a square,leaving a thickness 3 to 4 cm in the middle, place the butter on the thick part.

Even out the butter with the palm of your hand, and fold over the rest of the dough to cover the butter completely.

Roll the block out to obtain a rectangle about 50 cm long by 20 cm wide, then fold one side to the centre, and do the same with the other side.

Turn the block and repeat the above, then put the dough in the refrigerator for 1 hour.

Repeat the rolling out and turning twice to obtain a 4-turn puff pastry. Leave to rest for another hour.

Roll out the pastry onto the baking tray to about 3 mm thick, to cover the tray. Trim the excess using a knife, without squashing the pastry.

Peel and core the apples, cut in half then into thin slices 2 mm thick and arrange these slices on the pastry to look like fish scales.

Sprinkle with sugar, put in a preheated oven (mark 7 /200°C) for 30 minutes.

Cook until the edges of the apples start to brown, then remove from the oven and leave to cool.

Glaze the tart with a little apricot jam (warmed and thinned with a little water).

LE RÉCAMIER

# SOUFFLÉ DE RIZ

## RICE SOUFFLÉ

Preparation **10 min** Cooking time **30 min** Equipment **soufflé mould**

SERVES 6

2 dessertspoons rice
1/2 l milk
2 dessertspoons caster sugar
1/2 vanilla pod
3 eggs
butter for the mould

Cook the rice in the milk to which sugar and vanilla have been added for 20 minutes, stirring often.

As soon as the rice is cooked, add the egg yolks one by one stirring constantly.

Beat the whites to firm peaks, then fold gradually and carefully into the rice.

Grease the mould well, pour in the mixture and cook in a preheated moderate oven (mark 6 /180°C) for 30 minutes.

Serve immediately.

# TARTE À LA RHUBARBE

## RHUBARB TART

Preparation **20 min** Cooking time **45 min** Equipment **ovenproof tart dish**

SERVES 6

| | |
|---|---|
| 250 g shortcrust pastry | 100 g hazelnuts |
| 1 kg pink rhubarb | 5 egg whites |
| 200 g caster sugar | icing sugar |

Prepare shortcrust pastry, put aside in a cool place.

Make a slightly sweet purée with the rhubarb, then drain well. Blanch the hazelnuts and crush by hand or in a food processor.

Line the dish with the pastry, and pour in the fruit purée to half-full. Beat the egg whites to firm peaks, add sugar and fold into the purée. Sprinkle with nuts and icing sugar.

Cook in a preheated low oven (mark 4 /140°C) for 45 minutes.

Leave to cool out of the oven, serve warm.

# TARTOUILLAT

Preparation **15 min** Cooking time **30 min** Equipment **tart mould**

SERVES 6

300 g flour
a pinch of salt
1/2 l milk
50 g sugar
2 large apples
125 g stoned cherries
butter to grease the mould

Mix the flour and milk, add the sugar and salt and beat well to a smooth consistency, obtaining a batter similar to that for pancakes.

Peel the apples and cut into rings. Mix the apples and stoned cherries into the batter. There should be plenty of fruit so that it is only just covered by the batter.

Grease the mould well and pour in the batter. Cook in a preheated moderate oven (mark 6 /180°C) for 30 minutes.

Serve quite hot.

*This is a common dessert in the Cluny area and used to be cooked on a cabbage leaf.*

# POIRES AU VIN DIJONNAISE

## DIJON PEARS IN WINE

Preparation **20 min** Cooking time **3 to 5 min** Equipment **small pan**

SERVES 4

4 pears
75 cl red Burgundy wine
cinnamon
vanilla essence
2 cloves
15 cl Crème de Cassis (blackcurrant liqueur)
250 g caster sugar
250 g apricot jelly

Pour the wine into the pan, add the cinnamon, vanilla and cloves.

Bring to the boil, soak the pears one by one for 2 minutes, then wash under cold water and peel. Cut into halves, and remove cores if necessary. Put aside.

Meanwhile, pour the blackcurrant liqueur into the wine which has been kept at simmering point. Add the sugar, mix well and leave to boil for 1 or 2 minutes.

Next, cook the pear halves for a few minutes according to the ripeness and quality of the pears. They must be cooked but still remain firm.

Remove the pears, leave to cool.

Reduce the cooking juices, adding the apricot jelly until the mixture becomes creamy and smooth.

Coat the pears with the sauce and serve.

*This dessert can be served hot or cold.*

# TOURTE AUX POMMES

## APPLE PUDDING

Preparation **20 min** Cooking time **35 min** Equipment **ovenproof dish with a lid**

Serves 6

| | |
|---|---|
| 1 kg apples | 12 slices of bread |
| 100 g honey | 1 teaspoon of cinnamon |
| 50 g granulated sugar | butter for the bread (about 100 g) |

Butter the bread thickly, then arrange 6 slices butter-side down in the dish.

Peel and core the apples, cut into rings and place on the slices of bread. Make layers of apples to a total thickness of 5 cm, sprinkling each layer with granulated sugar and a little cinnamon.

Then cover the apples with the 6 other slices of bread, buttered side towards the apples and spread with honey on the top.

Put on the lid and place in a preheated low oven (mark 5 /170°C) for 35 minutes.

Cook until well caramelized. Serve hot as a dessert, but not scalding.

# TOT-FAIT

Preparation **10 min** Cooking time **25 min** Equipment **deep sandwich tin**

SERVES 4

60 g flour
3 eggs
1/4 l milk
3 dessertspoons granulated sugar
1 dessertspoon coffee extract
1 sachet vanilla sugar
butter to grease the mould

Mix the egg yolks and flour in a thick-based saucepan using a wooden spatula.

Over a low heat, stirring constantly, pour in the milk slowly, add the sugar, vanilla sugar, and coffee extract and leave to thicken.

Beat the egg whites into firm peaks then fold carefully into the mixture. Grease the mould, pour in the mixture and sprinkle with caster sugar.

Place in a preheated hot oven (mark 7 / 200°C) for 20 to 25 minutes.

Leave to cool when removed from the oven and serve warm as a dessert.

# Index of wines and recipes

## White wines

Pernand-Vergelesses 1992
P. Dubreuil-Fontaine Père et Fils
Tête de veau à la bourguignonne, p 84

Pouilly-Fuissé - Château Fuissé 1991
J.J. Vincent et Fils
Ecrevisses au vin blanc, p 22
Pâté de veau de Bourg, p 74

Pouilly-Fuissé - Château Fuissé les Brûlés
J.J. Vincent et Fils
Anguille bourguignonne, p 27
Saucisson de Lyon, p 80

Pouilly-Fuissé -Cuvée vieilles vignes 1993
Roger Lassarat
Gateau salé de Dôle, p 30

Puligny-Montrachet 1er cru
Clos de la Mouchère 1992
J. Boillot
Escargots à la bourguignonne, p 27
Fricassée de poulet à la crème, p 94
Petits poulets à la beaunoise, p 102
Raie à la moutarde, p 123

Puligny-Montrachet - Les Combettes 1992
Domaine J. Prieur
Salade de truffes fraîches, p 40

Puligny-Montrachet 1992
Les Combettes
Etienne Sauzet
Filets de brochet dijonnaise, p 118
Pintade à la matelotte, p 98
Poularde de bresse demi-deuil, p 104

Rully - Chateau de Rully 1992
Antonin Rodet
Le jambon persillé, p 32
Raie à la moutarde, p 123

Rully - Château de Rully 1989
Antonin Rodet
Mousse de brochet, p 116

Rully - Château de Rully 1986
Antonin Rodet
Cassolette d'escargots, p 26
Fricassée de poulet à la crème, p 94

Santenay 1991 - Clos de Malte
Louis Jadot
Poulet aux girolles, p 103

## Red wines

Beaune Clos des Marconnets 1988
Chanson Père et Fils
Côtes d'agneau champvallon, p 62
Quasi de veau en cocotte, p 79

Beaune Clos des Mouches 1991
Joseph Drouhin
Faisan auc châtaignes, p 95
Perdreaux aux morilles, p 99

Beaune Bressandes 1988
Chanson Père et Fils
Potée Bourguignonne, p 76

Bonnes-Mares 1989
Joseph Drouhin
Cuissot de sanglier rôti, p 87
Sauté de boeuf bourguignon, p 82

Bourgogne Pinot Noir Vieilles vignes 1990
Antonin Rodet
Fondue bourguignonne, p 70
Pauchouse, p 125

Chambolle-Musigny 1991
Domaine J. Prieur
Pâté de tête de marcassin, p 39

Chambolle-Musigny 1990
Domaine Arlaud Père et Fils
Poulet aux girolles, p 103
Râble de lièvre à la crème, p 106

Chassagne-Montrachet 1er Cru 1990
Dom. des Htes Cornières Chapelle et Fils
Rôti de marcassin, p 107

Clos Vougeot 1991
Domaine J. Prieur
Coq sauté aux vins de Bourgogne, p 91
Sauté de boeuf bourguignon, p 82
Poitrine de veau en meurette, p 78

Corton Bressandes 1991
Domaine J. Prieur
Lapin à la beaunoise, p 89
Pintade aux lentilles, p 96

Gevrey-Chambertin 1992
Domaine Armand Rousseau Père et fils
Meurette de bourgogne, p 121

# Index of wines and recipes

# Contents

Photographs :
CHRISTIAN CRAMPONT (cover and recipes)
GEORGES GARCIN, page 36
SUNSET, pages 56, 100
DOMINIQUE PERNIN, page 65

Printed in May 1999
by EUROGRAFICA - Vicenza
Layout MIREILLE VEYSSIÈRE
Gravure SYNAPSE in Brive


Rue Droite près l'Eglise - 46600 Martel
Tél (33 05) 65 37 43 54  Fax (33 05) 65 37 43 55

ISBN 2-910333-24-8
ISSN 1242-5249
Dépôt légal n° 950359-4